ngmacaroni
uesandwich
ettekabobs
cakesstirfry
chedfritters
atedpizza

the
quick
and easy
book

Published by Fog City Press
814 Montgomery Street
San Francisco, CA 94133 USA

Copyright © 2002 Weldon Owen Pty Ltd

Chief Executive Officer: John Owen
President: Terry Newell
Publisher: Lynn Humphries
Managing Editor: Janine Flew
Art Director: Kylie Mulquin
Editorial Coordinator: Tracey Gibson
Editorial Assistant: Kiren Thandi
Production Manager: Caroline Webber
Production Coordinator: James Blackman
Sales Manager: Emily Jahn
Vice President International Sales: Stuart Laurence
European Sales Director: Vanessa Mori

Project Editor: Janine Flew
Project Designer: Jacqueline Richards
Food Photography: Valerie Martin
Food Stylist: Sally Parker
Home Economist: Christine Sheppard

ISBN 1 876778 98 9

Color reproduction by SC (Sang Choy) International Pte Ltd
Manufactured by Kyodo Printing Co. (S'pore) Pte Ltd
Printed in Singapore

A Weldon Owen Production

the
quick
and easy
book

FOG CITY PRESS

contents

good food fast

Most people love to eat, and try to eat well, but not everyone has the time or inclination to spend hours in the kitchen. But even when our busy lives give us less time for cooking, our diets and palates needn't suffer. To produce good meals in minutes, you just need to remember a couple of simple points. One is to use the best possible ingredients, and not do too much to them—instead, let their quality and freshness speak for themselves. Another is to be organized and think ahead. When you're making pasta sauce, for example, make a double batch and freeze half for later. Or, when you have a spare few hours, make a big pot of stock and freeze it in small portions. And be sure your pantry is always well stocked with staples such as pasta, rice, and tinned goods, as well as the many good-quality convenience foods that are widely available these days. Using such foods isn't cheating—it's a practical way to put together a nourishing, delicious meal in minimum time. The following pages detail some of the most useful foods to keep on hand for quick and easy cooking.

pasta This extremely versatile ingredient is available in a vast array of sizes and shapes, both dried and fresh. Dried pasta keeps for months, cooks in minutes, and can feed a crowd very economically. Fresh pasta, which cooks even more quickly, is best used soon after purchase, but may be frozen in small portions. Have on hand several types to suit various dishes. Long pasta strands, such as spaghetti, linguine, and fettuccine, go well with creamy sauces. Small to medium shapes, such as farfalle, penne, and fusilli, suit robust, chunky sauces. Tiny pasta, such as orzo, is added to soups. Filled pastas, such as ravioli and tortellini, need only a simple sauce and a crisp green salad to be a complete meal. Couscous, although it looks like a grain, is actually a North African form of pasta made from semolina. Most supermarkets stock an "instant" version; just add boiling water, cover the pan, and leave for about 5 minutes for the couscous to swell and soften. Use it to accompany meat or vegetable stews and casseroles.

pasta sauces Many good commercial sauces are available, both creamy and tomato-based. A plain tomato pasta sauce (the type sold in Italian stores may be labelled "sugo") is particularly versatile. Warmed and poured over cooked pasta, it provides an instant meal. With such additions as meat, vegetables, and herbs, it becomes a more substantial sauce. It can also be used to flavor other dishes, such as pizzas or casseroles. When you have time, cook up a big batch of homemade sauce and freeze some in small portions for later.

noodles These Asian staples are made from rice, wheat, or bean flour, and are available fresh or dried. Types include buckwheat (soba), egg noodles, mung bean noodles (known under various names, including cellophane noodles, glass noodles, or bean thread noodles), rice noodles of various sizes, and different types of wheat noodles, such as soba, somen, and udon. Fresh or dried noodles are generally boiled before they are used, though some thin varieties only need to be soaked in hot water. Dried noodles are sometimes fried, without first being soaked, to create feathery, crisp threads. Serve noodles with stir-fried meats, seafood, and vegetables, or in Asian-style soups.

canned fish is widely available and very convenient for use in sandwiches, salads, or mornays, or with pasta. Tuna and salmon are both available packed in oil, water, or brine. They may be plain or have added flavors, such as basil or other herbs, lemon pepper, chile, or sun-dried tomato. Anchovy fillets, when cooked in pasta sauces and stews, lose their fishy pungency, enhancing other flavors and giving depth and zest.

canned, jarred, and frozen vegetables
Look for cans or jars of artichoke hearts, sun-dried tomatoes, sun-dried bell peppers (capsicums), baby corn, olives, baby beets, and various types of beans and lentils. Use them on sandwiches and melts, in soups, chopped in pasta sauce, tossed in a stir-fry, or with vegetables, cold meats, and olives as part of a quick antipasto plate. Canned beans and lentils are already cooked, and need only be rinsed before being added to recipes. Canned tomatoes are indispensable in stews, soups, and pasta sauces. Stir-fries and salads require fresh vegetables, but frozen vegetables are useful standbys for soups and casseroles, and to accompany meat, poultry, and fish dishes when fresh produce is not in season.

condiments such as mustards, vinegars, and commercial sauces add zest to all types of foods. Vinegars, such as balsamic or wine vinegars, are essential for salad dressings. Worcestershire sauce, Thai or Vietnamese fish sauce, hot-pepper sauce (such as Tabasco), and ketchup (tomato sauce) can be added to recipes or used as dipping sauces. A selection of mustards, such as Dijon, seeded, or hot English, is useful for sandwiches or salad dressings.

stock and soup bases Stock forms the basis of many good soups, stews, risottos, and sauces. Make a big batch and freeze it in small portions, or keep commercial stocks in the pantry. Canned consommé, diluted with water, can be used instead of stock. A commercial stock will be improved in flavor if simmered for even 15–20 minutes with a few vegetables and some fresh herbs.

cheese Keep a few different types of cheese in your refrigerator. A grating cheese, such as Parmesan, perks up pasta and adds flavor to stews, soups, and risottos. A sharp or mild cheese, such as Cheddar or Gouda, is good for sandwiches. A melting cheese, such as Mozzarella, can be used on pizzas and melts. A soft cheese, such as cream cheese, can be spread on sandwiches or used in desserts.

pastry, dough, and bread Good-quality frozen pastry is readily available, either ready-rolled or in a block that you can roll out to the desired size and shape. Or buy ready-baked pastry cases and add your own filling. Purchased pizza bases are handy, too—just spread some tomato paste over, top with chopped sun-dried vegetables, sliced salami or ham, and shredded cheese, then bake. Many supermarkets also stock preshaped bread dough that is ready to be baked at home, giving the delicious treat of warm, fragrant bread without the time and hassle of mixing and kneading the dough and then waiting for it to rise.

herbs These fragrant, flavorful plants are indispensable in the kitchen. Just a small amount of them can have a huge effect on a dish. Basil complements soups, stews, salads, and pastas; tarragon is a classic partner for chicken; cilantro (fresh coriander) is associated with Mexican and Asian cuisines. Fresh herbs give the best flavor, but many dried herbs are also good.

preserved fruits For eating out of hand, fresh fruit is always best, but preserved fruits are delicious for baking and desserts. Use them straight from the can or jar for breakfast, alone or atop cereal; with cream, yogurt, or ice cream for dessert; or piled into a homemade or purchased tart shell. Many fruits are also available frozen; frozen berries, in particular, can be very good, especially for baking.

cookies aren't just for eating with milk or coffee. Try crushing amaretti (Italian almond cookies) over ice cream. Savoiardi (sponge fingers/ladyfingers) can accompany ice cream, form the basis of tiramisu, or be dusted with confectioner's (icing) sugar to partner fresh fruits. Crushed cookies, such as gingersnaps, biscotti, or chocolate wafers, mixed with melted butter and pressed into a pie plate or springform pan, can be the basis of a sweet pie or cheese-cake. Do the same with graham crackers (wholemeal biscuits) for an alternative to a savory pastry crust.

quick and easy
breakfast
treats

homemade
muesli

makes about 2 lb (1 kg)

3 cups (9 oz/280 g) regular rolled oats

2 cups (10 oz/315 g) coarse oat bran

¾ cup (2 oz/60 g) unsweetened dried grated
(desiccated) coconut

⅓ cup (2 oz/60 g) dried currants

⅓ cup (2 oz/60 g) golden raisins (sultanas)

¼ cup (1 oz/30 g) chopped dried mango

⅓ cup (1½ oz/45 g) chopped dried apple

⅓ cup (1½ oz/45 g) chopped dried apricots

½ cup (2 oz/60 g) chopped almonds

¼ cup (1 oz/30 g) chopped raw cashews

⅓ cup (2½ oz/75 g) pumpkin seeds (pepitas)

⅓ cup (2½ oz/75 g) sunflower seeds

¼ cup (1½ oz/45 g) linseed

◈ Combine all the ingredients
in a large bowl and mix well.

◈ Serve with milk, yogurt,
honey, berries, or other fruit.

◈ The muesli will keep in
an airtight container for up
to 1 month.

buttermilk and banana waffles

makes 7 waffles; serves 3–4

Waffles were first prepared in France and Belgium during the Middle Ages. This batter incorporates buttermilk for tenderness and a delicious tang, and mashed ripe bananas for moisture and sweetness.

1 cup (5 oz/155 g) all-purpose (plain) flour

1 tablespoon sugar

1 teaspoon baking powder

1/2 teaspoon baking soda (bicarbonate of soda)

1/2 teaspoon ground cinnamon

1/4 teaspoon salt

1 1/2 cups (10 fl oz/315 ml) buttermilk

1 egg

2 tablespoons unsalted butter, melted

2 ripe bananas, peeled and sliced

vegetable oil

maple syrup, warmed

◈ In a large bowl, stir together the flour, sugar, baking powder, baking soda, cinnamon, and salt, mixing well.

◈ In a large measuring cup, combine the buttermilk, egg, and melted butter and whisk until blended. Place half of the sliced bananas in a small bowl and mash coarsely; do not worry if the mixture is a little lumpy. Add the mashed banana to the buttermilk mixture, then stir the liquid into the flour mixture. Using a fork or whisk, mix until the batter is smooth.

◈ Preheat a waffle iron according to the manufacturer's directions.

◈ Using a paper towel or pastry brush, lightly grease the waffle iron with vegetable oil. Following the manufacturer's directions, ladle batter sufficient for 1 waffle into the iron, spreading it evenly.

◈ Close the waffle iron and cook until the waffle iron will open easily (no peeking for the first 2 minutes). Transfer the waffle to a platter and keep warm while you cook the remaining batter.

◈ Serve the waffles garnished with the remaining banana slices and drizzled with the warmed maple syrup.

strawberry-topped
french toast

French toast, known in France as *pain perdu*, or "lost bread," was originally designed as a way to use up day-old bread. Although all types of bread now go into this breakfast classic, many cooks still opt for day-old slices, relying on the egg and milk for moisture.

¾ cup (7½ oz/235 g) strawberry preserves or jam

½ cup (2 oz/60 g) strawberries, hulled

water, as needed

4 eggs

1½ cups (12 fl oz/375 ml) milk

1 teaspoon vanilla extract (essence)

½ teaspoon finely grated orange zest

1 tablespoon sugar

8 slices egg bread or sourdough bread

3 tablespoons unsalted butter

In a blender or a food processor fitted with the metal blade, combine the strawberry preserves or jam and the strawberries. Purée, scraping down the sides of the blender or food processor bowl from time to time. Add a little water, if needed, to form a syrupy consistency. Set aside.

In a bowl, whisk together the eggs, milk, vanilla, orange zest, and sugar until well blended. Working in batches if necessary, arrange the bread slices in a single layer in a baking dish with 2-inch (5-cm) sides. Pour the egg mixture over the bread slices and then turn them to coat evenly. Let the bread stand for 5 minutes, or a little longer if you like custardy French toast.

In a large nonstick frying pan over medium heat, melt 1½ tablespoons of the butter. When the foam subsides, add half of the bread slices in a single layer and cook the bread until golden brown on the first side, 2–4 minutes. Turn the slices and cook on the second side until golden, about 2 minutes longer. (For drier toasts, cook them for 1–2 minutes longer after they turn golden.) Transfer to warmed individual plates, cover loosely with aluminum foil, and keep warm. Repeat with the remaining butter and bread.

Serve immediately, drizzled with the strawberry syrup.

golden raisin–bran muffins

makes 12 standard muffins

Soaking the bran cereal in the liquid ingredients until it is fully plumped gives these muffins a wonderfully moist texture. For best results, select an unprocessed bran cereal such as All Bran or Bran Buds.

2 eggs

$\frac{1}{3}$ cup (2$\frac{1}{2}$ oz/75 g) firmly packed light or dark brown sugar

$\frac{1}{2}$ cup (4 fl oz/125 ml) vegetable oil

2 cups (16 fl oz/500 ml) buttermilk

$\frac{1}{2}$ teaspoon salt

1$\frac{1}{2}$ cups (4 oz/125 g) wheat bran cereal (see note)

2$\frac{1}{4}$ cups (11 oz/360 g) all-purpose (plain) flour

2 teaspoons baking soda (bicarbonate of soda)

$\frac{3}{4}$ cup (4$\frac{1}{2}$ oz/140 g) golden raisins (sultanas)

Preheat an oven to 400°F (200°C/Gas Mark 5). Generously butter twelve ½-cup (4-fl oz/125-ml) muffin-tin cups.

In a large bowl, combine the eggs, brown sugar, vegetable oil, buttermilk, salt, and bran cereal. Using a wooden spoon, mix well. Let rest for at least 10 minutes or up to 1 hour to soften the bran.

In another bowl, stir together the flour and baking soda. Add the milk mixture to the flour mixture, stirring until just combined. Do not overmix. Stir in the raisins.

Spoon the batter into the prepared muffin cups, filling each cup two-thirds full. Bake until golden, about 20 minutes. Do not overcook.

Transfer the pan to a rack and let cool for 15 minutes. Turn out the muffins onto the rack and serve warm or at room temperature.

Wrap any cooled leftover muffins airtight and store at room temperature for up to 2 days.

recipe hint

Muffin recipes always specify the size of the pans to be used, but you can change the size of the pans if you adjust the baking time. A recipe for 12 standard muffins will make about 6 large muffins or 24 mini muffins.

Standard muffins are about 2½ inches (6 cm) in diameter and have a ½-cup (4-fl oz) capacity. They usually take about 15 minutes to cook.

Large muffins are 3 inches (8 cm) in diameter, with a 1-cup (8-fl oz) capacity, and take about 20 minutes to cook.

Mini muffins are 1¾ inches (4.5 cm), with a ¼-cup (2-fl oz) capacity, and take about 12 minutes to cook.

african
fruit salad

*1 large papaya
(pawpaw), at least
1 lb (500 g),
halved, seeded,
and peeled*

*2 mangoes, about
1 lb (500 g) each*

*1 large pineapple,
3–4 lb (1.5–2 kg)*

2 large bananas

◈ Dice the papaya flesh. Place in a large serving bowl.

◈ Peel the mangoes. Slice as much of the flesh off the pit as possible, being careful to capture any juices. Dice the flesh and add, along with the juices, to the bowl holding the papaya.

◈ Using a sturdy, sharp knife, cut off the top and bottom of the pineapple. Set the pineapple upright on a cutting board. Working from top to bottom, slice off the skin. Cut out any remaining eyes or dark spots. Cut the pineapple lengthwise into quarters, then cut lengthwise again to remove the tough inner core on each quarter. Dice the flesh into small cubes, again being careful to capture any juices. Add the pineapple and juices to the other fruits. Toss well, cover, and refrigerate until well chilled.

◈ Just before serving, peel and dice the bananas. Add to the bowl, toss well, and serve.

oat and barley
cereal

serves 6

2½ cups (20 fl oz/625 ml) water

1 cup (8 fl oz/250 ml) milk, plus
extra to serve (optional)

1 cup (3 oz/90 g) regular
rolled oats

1 cup (3 oz/90 g) quick-cooking
barley or barley flakes

3 tablespoons packed
brown sugar

¾ teaspoon ground cinnamon

⅛ teaspoon salt

3 oz (90 g) chopped dried fruit
such as dates, apricots, apples,
pears, prunes, or raisins

◈ In a large saucepan over medium heat, combine
the water and milk. Bring to a boil, then stir in the
oats, barley, brown sugar, cinnamon, and salt.

◈ Return to a boil, then reduce heat, cover, and
simmer for 5 minutes.

◈ Stir in the dried fruit and cook for about 7 minutes
longer, or until the barley is tender. Serve hot with milk,
if desired, or cover and refrigerate to serve later.

sour cream pancakes

makes about sixteen 4-inch (10-cm) pancakes; serves 4

These light-textured pancakes are perfect for topping with seasonal fruits, such as boysenberries, blueberries, or nectarines. Out of season, use well-drained frozen fruit or even fruit preserves. A little grated lemon zest sprinkled over the top at the last minute makes a fresh and tangy garnish.

¾ cup (4 oz/125 g) all-purpose (plain) flour

¼ cup (⅔ oz/20 g) quick-cooking (instant) rolled oats

1 tablespoon sugar

1 teaspoon baking powder

½ teaspoon baking soda (bicarbonate of soda)

½ teaspoon ground cinnamon

¼ teaspoon salt

½ cup (4 fl oz/125 ml) buttermilk

1 cup (8 fl oz/250 ml) sour cream

1 egg

2 tablespoons unsalted butter, melted

vegetable oil

blueberry syrup or other fruit syrup, warmed

fresh or frozen fruits or fruit preserves (optional)

✧ In a large bowl, stir together the flour, rolled oats, sugar, baking powder, baking soda, cinnamon, and salt, mixing well.

✧ In a large measuring cup, combine the buttermilk, sour cream, egg, and melted butter. Using a fork, beat until well blended. Add the buttermilk mixture to the flour mixture and mix well with the fork or a whisk to form a smooth batter.

✧ Place a griddle or large nonstick frying pan over medium-high heat. When a drop of water sprinkled on top skitters across the surface, lightly grease the surface with vegetable oil.

✧ For each pancake, pour about ¼ cup (2 fl oz/60 ml) of the batter onto the hot surface; do not crowd the surface. Cook until little bubbles appear on the tops of the pancakes, 3–5 minutes. Using a spatula, turn them and cook on the second side until both sides are equally browned, 1–2 minutes longer. Transfer the pancakes to a platter and keep warm in a low oven while you cook the remaining batter in the same way.

✧ To serve, drizzle the pancakes with warmed fruit syrup, garnish with fruit, if desired, and serve at once.

fruit frappé

*3 cups (1 lb/500 g) cut-up
banana, mango, strawberries,
and/or papaya (pawpaw),
in any combination
(1½-inch/4-cm chunks)*

*1 cup (8 fl oz/250 ml) orange,
pineapple, grapefruit, or
cranberry juice, or as needed*

*1 cup (8 fl oz/250 ml)
strawberry, lemon, lime,
passionfruit, or raspberry
frozen yogurt or sherbet
(low-fat, non-fat, or regular)*

❖ Place the fruit, juice, and frozen yogurt or sherbet in a blender. Purée until smooth, adding additional juice if desired for a thinner consistency.

❖ Pour into four tall glasses and serve immediately.

tropical papaya boats

serves 4

2 papayas (pawpaws), each
about 6 inches (15 cm) long

juice of 1 small lime

2 kiwifruits, peeled and
sliced crosswise

1 cup (6 oz/185 g) fresh
pineapple chunks

1 mango

1 banana, peeled and
sliced crosswise

❖ Cut the papayas in half lengthwise; scoop out and discard the seeds. Set one half on each individual plate, hollow side up. Sprinkle evenly with the lime juice.

❖ Arrange the kiwifruit slices and pineapple chunks attractively in the papaya halves.

❖ Peel the mango. Cut the flesh lengthwise off the pit in thick slices, cutting as close to the pit as possible.

❖ Add the mango slices and banana slices to the papaya halves and serve.

quick and easy
soups, snacks, *and* light meals

garlic shrimp

1/4 cup (2 fl oz/60 ml) olive oil

*4 large cloves garlic,
finely minced*

1 teaspoon red pepper flakes

*1 lb (500 g) uncooked medium
shrimp (prawns), peeled
and deveined*

2 tablespoons fresh lemon juice

2 tablespoons dry sherry

1 teaspoon paprika

salt and ground black pepper

*chopped fresh flat-leaf (Italian)
parsley, to garnish*

❖ In a large frying pan over medium heat, warm the olive oil. Add the garlic and red pepper flakes and sauté for 1 minute.

❖ Raise the heat to high and add the shrimp, lemon juice, sherry, and paprika. Stir well, then sauté, stirring briskly, until the shrimp turn pink and curl up, about 3 minutes.

❖ Season with salt and pepper to taste and sprinkle with the parsley. Serve immediately.

croque-monsieur

serves 4

8 slices dense-textured white sandwich bread

½ cup (4 oz/125 g) unsalted butter, at room temperature

10 oz (300 g) Gruyère cheese, thinly sliced

5 oz (150 g) cooked ham, thinly sliced

cornichons (French-style pickles) (optional)

Dijon mustard (optional)

◈ Lightly coat one side of each bread slice with some of the butter. Layer half of the Gruyère slices on the unbuttered side of four of the bread slices. Top with the ham, dividing it evenly among the slices, then with the remaining Gruyère. Place the remaining bread slices, buttered sides up, atop the cheese.

◈ Place a large nonstick frying pan over medium heat. When it is hot, slip a sandwich into the pan and cook until golden brown on the bottom, 1½–2 minutes. Using a spatula, turn the sandwich over and continue to cook, reducing the heat slightly, until golden brown on the bottom and the cheese has melted, about 2 minutes longer. Transfer to a warmed platter and repeat with the remaining sandwiches. If necessary, the sandwiches can be reheated for 2–3 minutes in a preheated 350°F (180°C/Gas Mark 4) oven.

◈ Serve hot, with cornichons and Dijon mustard, if desired.

hot and sour
shrimp soup

1 tablespoon vegetable oil

1 cup (4 oz/125 g) chopped onion

1 small fresh green chile, seeded and finely chopped

1-inch (2.5-cm) piece fresh ginger, peeled and chopped

2 oz (60 g) small oyster mushrooms

4 cups (32 fl oz/1 liter) chicken stock

1 stalk lemongrass, cut into 4 pieces

1 tablespoon white wine vinegar

1 lb (500 g) large uncooked shrimp (prawns), peeled and roughly chopped

juice of 1 lime

salt and ground black pepper

❖ Heat the oil in a large frying pan over medium heat and cook the onion, chile, and ginger for 4–5 minutes. Add the mushrooms and fry for 1–2 minutes more.

❖ Stir in the stock, lemongrass, and vinegar. Bring to a boil, then reduce the heat, cover, and simmer for 10–12 minutes.

❖ Add the shrimp and simmer until they turn pink, about 2 minutes more. Remove the lemongrass, add the lime juice and salt and pepper to taste, and serve at once.

super salsas

S alsa is Spanish for "sauce," and describes any number of chunky relishes, often with a tomato base and seasoned with chile. Salsas make a handy basis for a quick snack or light meal. Try them dolloped on bread or crackers, used as a dip for corn chips or sticks of fresh raw vegetables, as an accompaniment to meat, fish, or chicken, or as a tangy garnish for soup. Use hot or mild chiles, depending on your palate. Leave the seeds in if you like extra heat.

mexican salsa

6 ripe medium tomatoes

2 fresh green chiles, seeded if desired, chopped

4 sprigs fresh oregano

1/2 medium onion, minced

1/2 tablespoon chopped cilantro (fresh coriander)

2 cloves garlic, minced

salt

✥ Put the tomatoes in a hot skillet to crack the skins. Cook for 2–4 minutes to reduce the tomato juice slightly. Allow to cool, then peel. Finely chop the flesh.

✥ In a bowl, combine the tomatoes with the chile, oregano, onion, cilantro, garlic, and salt to taste. Mix well.

✥ Use immediately, or spoon into sterilized jars and seal tightly. Store in the refrigerator for 3–5 days.

makes 2 cups (1 lb/500 g)

cherry tomato salsa

1 lb (500 g) cherry tomatoes

1 large golden (French) shallot, minced

1 clove garlic, minced

2 tablespoons chopped cilantro
(fresh coriander)

1 tablespoon white wine vinegar

2 teaspoons fresh lime juice

2 fresh green or red chiles, seeded
if desired, chopped

salt and pepper

❖ In a food processor, process the
tomatoes to a coarse consistency.

❖ Transfer the tomatoes and their juice to
a bowl. Mix in the shallot, garlic, cilantro,
vinegar, lime juice, chile, and salt and
pepper to taste.

❖ Cover and refrigerate, letting the flavors
meld for at least 2 hours.

❖ Store in the refrigerator for 2–3 days.

makes 1 lb (500 g)

tomatillo salsa

3 fresh green chiles, seeded if desired, halved

1 onion, quartered

1 clove garlic, quartered

2 tablespoons minced cilantro (fresh
coriander)

20 tomatillos (about 22 oz/700 g), husked,
washed, and heated until tender

1/2 teaspoon sugar

salt and pepper

2 tablespoons olive oil

❖ In a food processor, finely chop the chiles,
onion, and garlic. Add the cilantro, tomatillos,
sugar, and salt and pepper to taste. Process
to the desired consistency.

❖ In a saucepan over medium heat, warm
the oil. Add the puréed ingredients and cook
for about 5 minutes. Do not allow to burn.

❖ Use immediately, or spoon into sterilized
jars and seal tightly. Store in the refrigerator
for 6–7 days.

makes 3 cups (2 lb/1 kg)

anchovy toasts

4 slices country-style bread,
cut ½ inch (1 cm) thick

1 clove garlic, cut in half
(optional)

extra-virgin olive oil

1 large, very ripe tomato

48 oil-packed anchovy fillets

ground black pepper

◈ Lightly toast the bread. If desired, rub the cut side of the garlic clove over the bread. Brush with olive oil.

◈ Cut the tomato in halves. Rub the halves over one side of each bread slice to coat it with the tomato juice and pulp.

◈ Arrange 12 drained anchovy fillets diagonally on each piece of toast. Sprinkle with pepper to taste, cut in halves, and serve at once.

blue cheese pizza

serves 2–4

1 large (9¹/₂-inch/24-cm)
pita bread pocket, piece
of lavash bread, or purchased
pizza base

¹/₂ cup (4 fl oz/125 ml)
homemade or purchased
tomato pasta sauce

3¹/₂ oz (100 g) blue cheese,
such as Roquefort, crumbled

¹/₃ cup (1³/₄ oz/50 g)
walnut pieces

◈ Preheat oven to 450°F (230°C/Gas Mark 7).

◈ Place the bread or pizza base on a baking sheet.
Spread the tomato sauce over the surface, then
top with the crumbled cheese and the walnuts.

◈ Bake for 15 minutes, or until the pizza is golden
on the edges and crisp underneath. Serve at once.

flavored cheeses

mustard and port cheese

1 cup (4 oz/125 g) grated Cheddar cheese
¼ cup (2 oz/60 g) unsalted butter, chopped
¼ cup (2 oz/60 g) grain mustard
2 tablespoons port wine
1 tablespoon fennel seeds

❖ Place cheese, butter, mustard, and port in the bowl of a food processor and process until combined. Transfer mixture to a bowl and refrigerate until firm enough to roll. Shape mixture into a log shape and wrap cheese in plastic wrap. Using your hands, roll cheese into a neat log, and refrigerate until firm. Remove plastic from cheese and roll cheese in fennel seeds.

❖ Store, wrapped in plastic wrap, in the refrigerator, or freeze for longer storage.

makes about 2 cups (10 oz/300 g)

herb and garlic cheese

¾ cup (6 oz/180 g) grated Ambrosia cheese
¾ cup (6 oz/180 g) ricotta cheese
¾ cup (6 oz/180 g) cream cheese, chopped
2 small cloves garlic, crushed
½ cup (½ oz/15 g) chopped fresh chives
¼ cup (¼ oz/7 g) chopped fresh parsley
1 tablespoon chopped sage
2 tablespoons poppyseeds, or as needed

❖ Place cheeses and garlic in the bowl of a food processor and process until combined. Transfer cheese mixture to a bowl, add the herbs, and mix well. Shape mixture into walnut-sized balls. Chill until firm, then roll cheese balls in poppyseeds.

❖ Store in an airtight container in the refrigerator, or freeze for longer storage.

makes about 3 cups (20 oz/625 g)

date and pistachio cheese

2 cups (8 oz/250 g) shelled pistachios

1 1/2 cups (12 oz/375 g) cream cheese, chopped

1/3 cup (3 oz/90 g) unsalted butter

1/3 cup (3 oz/90 g) ricotta cheese

1 tablespoon honey

1 tablespoon brandy

1/2 cup (3 oz/90 g) chopped dates

❖ Place pistachios in the bowl of a food processor and process until finely chopped. Remove nuts from processor; set aside 1/4 cup (1 oz/30 g) for garnish. Place cream cheese, butter, ricotta, honey, and brandy in bowl of food processor and process until combined. Transfer mixture to a bowl, add the pistachios and dates, and mix well.

❖ Line an 8-inch (20-cm) cake pan with plastic wrap. Press mixture evenly into tin. Chill until firm. At serving time, turn cheese out onto a serving board, remove plastic wrap, and press on reserved pistachio nuts.

makes about 3 cups (20 oz/625 g)

pesto cheese

1 1/2 oz (45 g) toasted pine nuts

3/4 cup (3/4 oz/25 g) fresh basil leaves, washed and well dried

1 clove garlic, crushed

2 tablespoons olive oil

3/4 cup (6 oz/180 g) feta cheese, chopped

2 tablespoons grated Parmesan cheese

2 bocconcini, chopped

1/2 cup (4 oz/125 g) ricotta cheese

1/4 cup (2 oz/60 g) unsalted butter, chopped

1 tablespoon sour cream

❖ Place 2 tablespoons (1 oz/30 g) of the pine nuts, the basil, and garlic in the bowl of a food processor and process until puréed. Add the oil, cheeses, butter, and sour cream and process until combined.

❖ Line a bowl with dampened cheesecloth (muslin), spoon mixture into bowl, and chill until firm. At serving time, turn cheese out onto a serving board, remove cheesecloth, and sprinkle remaining pine nuts on top.

makes about 3 cups (20 oz/625 g)

thai-style chicken and coconut soup

serves 4 as a main course
or 8 as an appetizer

2 tablespoons vegetable oil

2 onions, chopped

3 cloves garlic, crushed

2 teaspoons ground cumin

1 teaspoon turmeric

1 teaspoon chopped fresh red or
green chile

1 tablespoon chopped fresh lemongrass

¼ cup (2 fl oz/60 ml) fresh lime juice

4 cups (32 fl oz/1 liter) chicken stock

2 cups (16 fl oz/500 ml) unsweetened
coconut milk

2 tablespoons Thai fish sauce

1 lb (500 g) boneless, skinless chicken
breasts, thinly sliced

2 tablespoons chopped cilantro
(fresh coriander)

lime leaves, to garnish (optional)

❖ Heat the oil in a large saucepan over low–medium heat, add the onion and garlic, and sauté, stirring, until the onion is soft, about 10 minutes.

❖ Add the cumin, turmeric, chile, and lemongrass and cook, stirring, until the lemongrass is tender, about 5 minutes more.

❖ Add the lime juice, stock, coconut milk, and fish sauce and bring to a boil. Stir in the chicken and simmer, uncovered, until the chicken is tender and no pink remains, about 3 minutes.

❖ Add the cilantro just before serving. Serve garnished with lime leaves, if desired.

❖ This recipe can be made a day ahead and gently reheated. Add the cilantro at the last minute.

recipe hint

Lemongrass (*Cymbopogon citratus*) is an aromatic herb used throughout Southeast Asia. It has long, thin leaves, a woody, ivory-colored stem tinged with pink, and a slightly bulbous base. The stalk and base are used to flavor soups, stews, and curries; the leaves may be used to make a refreshing infused tea. Powdered forms are available, but they have none of the fresh herb's lemony pungency. Lemongrass is available in supermarkets and Asian markets. Choose firm stalks with no sign of fading or drying. Remove the leaves and refrigerate the stalks in a plastic bag for up to 2 weeks.

serves 4

*16 slices (rashers)
thick-cut bacon*

*⅓ cup (3 fl oz/80 ml)
mayonnaise*

*2 teaspoons fresh
lemon juice*

¼ teaspoon salt

pinch of white pepper

*½ lb (250 g) cooked
turkey breast,
thinly sliced*

2 tomatoes, sliced

*8 large iceberg or
other lettuce leaves,
torn into pieces*

12 slices white bread

❖ In a large nonstick frying pan over medium heat, cook the bacon, turning once, until crisp, 4–6 minutes. Transfer to a plate lined with a double thickness of paper towels and set aside.

❖ In a small bowl, stir together the mayonnaise, lemon juice, salt, and pepper, mixing well.

❖ Assemble the bacon, lemon mayonnaise, turkey, tomatoes, and lettuce around you on a large work surface before you begin to make the sandwiches.

❖ Toast the bread slices until golden brown. Lay the toasted slices on the work surface and spread them evenly with the lemon mayonnaise. Top four of the bread slices with an equal amount of the turkey, followed by half of the lettuce. Top the lettuce with a second slice of bread, mayonnaise-side up. Place an equal number of tomato slices and then four bacon slices on each sandwich, and top with the rest of the lettuce. Top with the four remaining bread slices, mayonnaise-side down. Press down gently to compact the sandwiches; secure with toothpicks.

❖ To serve, using a serrated knife, slice into halves or quarters, then transfer to individual plates.

triple-decker
club sandwich

clear broth
with grilled seafood

serves 4–6

*6 cups (48 fl oz/1.5 l)
fish stock*

½ lb (250 g) sea scallops

*½ lb (250 g) uncooked
shrimp (prawns), peeled
and deveined*

*2 tablespoons unsalted
butter, melted*

salt and white pepper

*fresh chives, snipped into
1-inch (2.5-cm) lengths*

❖ Preheat a broiler (griller) or a gas or electric grill (barbecue) until very hot, or prepare a fire in a charcoal grill.

❖ In a saucepan, bring the fish stock to a boil over medium heat. Reduce the heat to very low and cover the pan.

❖ Meanwhile, brush the scallops and shrimp with melted butter and season lightly with salt and pepper. Place the seafood on an unheated broiler rack or grill rack and cook close to the heat source until well seared and barely cooked through, 1–2 minutes per side.

❖ When the seafood is almost done, ladle the hot stock into warmed large, shallow soup plates, taking care not to fill them all the way. Neatly place the pieces of seafood in the stock; they should protrude slightly above the surface of the liquid. Float the chives in the stock and serve immediately.

asparagus with dijon-herb mayonnaise

**serves 4 as an appetizer
or side dish**

DIJON-HERB MAYONNAISE

1 large egg

4 teaspoons fresh lemon juice

*1 tablespoon finely chopped
fresh basil or 1 teaspoon
dried basil, crushed*

*1 tablespoon finely chopped
fresh thyme or 1 teaspoon
dried thyme, crushed*

1 tablespoon Dijon mustard

½ teaspoon salt

*1 cup (8 fl oz/250 ml) extra-
virgin olive oil or salad oil*

1 lb (500 g) asparagus

❖ For the mayonnaise, in a blender or food processor, combine the egg, lemon juice, basil, thyme, mustard, and salt. Blend for 5 seconds. With the machine running at high speed, gradually add the oil in a fine stream through the feed tube or the hole in the lid, blending until smooth.

❖ Prepare the asparagus by bending each spear; discard the woody bases where the spears snap easily.

❖ Place the asparagus in the top of a double boiler or in a steamer basket over water in a saucepan. Cover and steam until crisp-tender, 5–6 minutes. Divide the spears among 4 serving plates; spoon over some of the mayonnaise.

❖ Any leftover mayonnaise may be refrigerated in an airtight container for up to 1 week.

bitter greens, blue cheese, and chicken sandwiches

serves 6

3 tablespoons (1½ oz/45 g) butter,
at room temperature

2 tablespoons sour cream

4 oz (125 g) blue Brie cheese, thinly sliced

6 large slices sourdough bread

24 endive and/or chicory leaves, or other
leaves of your choice

⅓ cup (3 fl oz/90 ml) extra-virgin olive oil

1 tablespoon lemon juice

1 teaspoon sugar

1 teaspoon grain mustard

8 oz (250 g) cooked chicken, sliced

1 small pear, thinly sliced

½ cup (2 oz/60 g) pecans, toasted

ground black pepper

❖ In a bowl, combine the butter, sour cream, and half the cheese. Beat with a wooden spoon until smooth and spreadable. Spread the cheese mixture onto the bread.

❖ In a screwtop jar, combine the olive oil, lemon juice, sugar, and mustard. Seal the jar and shake well. Pour the dressing over the salad leaves and toss well. Top the bread with the leaves and dressing, then with the chicken, remaining blue cheese, pear slices, and pecans. Sprinkle with pepper to taste and serve immediately.

smoked trout pâté

makes 1½ cups (12 oz/375 g)

4 oz (125 g) filleted smoked trout meat

2 tablespoons drained, prepared horseradish cream

⅓ cup (3 fl oz/90 ml) sour cream

¼ cup (2 fl oz/60 ml) heavy (double) cream

1 tablespoon capers

small toasts, baguette slices, or crackers, to serve

dill, to garnish (optional)

❖ In the bowl of a food processor, combine the smoked trout and horseradish cream. Process for 1 minute. Add the sour cream and heavy cream and process to combine. Stir in the capers.

❖ Serve on small toasts, fresh baguette slices, or crackers. Garnish with dill, if desired.

❖ Leftover pâté may be stored in the refrigerator, covered, for up to 3 days.

corn, shrimp, and bell pepper fritters

makes about 24

2 cups (12 oz/375 g) fresh corn kernels
(from about 3 large ears)

1/2 lb (250 g) uncooked shrimp (prawns),
peeled, deveined, and coarsely chopped

2 golden (French) shallots, finely chopped

1 small green or red bell pepper (capsicum),
or 1/2 of each, seeded and finely chopped

1 small fresh red chile, seeded and
finely minced

2 cloves garlic, finely chopped

1 egg

1/4 cup (1 1/4 oz/40 g) all-purpose (plain) flour

1/4 teaspoon baking soda (bicarbonate
of soda)

1 teaspoon ground coriander

1/2 teaspoon ground cumin

1 teaspoon salt

2 tablespoons water

peanut or corn oil, for frying

sriracha sauce or sweet chile sauce, for
dipping, or a squeeze of lime or lemon juice

◈ In a food processor fitted with the metal blade, process the corn to a coarse paste. (Do not purée.) Scrape the corn into a large bowl. Add the shrimp, shallot, bell pepper, chile, garlic, and egg; mix well. In a small bowl, stir together the flour, baking soda, coriander, cumin, salt, and water. Add to the corn mixture and mix well.

◈ In a large, heavy frying pan over medium–high heat, pour in oil to a depth of at least 1 inch (2.5 cm) and heat to about 375°F (190°C) on a deep-frying thermometer. Drop a few heaping tablespoonfuls of the corn mixture into the oil, leaving enough space for each fritter to spread. Fry until golden brown and crisp on the underside, about 1 minute. Turn over and continue to fry until brown and crisp on the second side, about 1 minute more. Using a slotted spoon, transfer the fritters to paper towels to drain. Place on a baking sheet and keep warm in a low oven while frying the remaining fritters.

◈ Serve the fritters hot or at room temperature with sriracha sauce, sweet chile sauce, or lime or lemon juice.

little tomato pizzas

makes 12

12 large slices dense-textured white bread

¼ cup (2 fl oz/60 ml) extra-virgin olive oil

12 oz (375 g) mozzarella cheese, thinly sliced

6 slices ham or prosciutto, halved

6 oz (180 g) cherry tomatoes, halved

6 drained, oil-packed anchovy fillets, chopped

2 teaspoons dried oregano

salt and ground black pepper

❖ Using a 3-inch (8-cm) round pastry cutter, cut a circle from each slice of bread.

❖ Use half the oil to brush one side of each round of bread. On each round, arrange a layer of cheese, a layer of ham or prosciutto, a layer of tomato, and a few pieces of anchovy. Sprinkle with oregano and season with salt and pepper to taste. Drizzle lightly with the remaining oil.

❖ Place the pizzas on a lightly oiled baking sheet and bake in a preheated 400°F (200°C/Gas Mark 5) oven until the cheese melts, about 10 minutes. Serve hot.

mussels
with cilantro
and tomato

serves 15 as cocktail food
or 5 as an appetizer

30 small mussels in their shells

3 tomatoes, peeled, seeded,
and chopped

salt and pepper

1 red bell pepper (capsicum),
finely chopped

1/3 cup (1/3 oz/10 g) finely
chopped cilantro (fresh
coriander)

1/4 cup (2 fl oz/60 ml)
balsamic vinegar

❖ Scrub the mussels, removing any beards that may still be attached. Steam until they just open; discard any that remain closed.

❖ Pull each mussel open, being careful not to tear the shell apart. Put a teaspoonful of tomato onto each mussel; season with salt and pepper to taste. Sprinkle with bell pepper and cilantro and finish with a small drizzle of balsamic vinegar.

❖ Serve hot or cold.

tuna melt

1 can (13 oz/410 g)
water-packed white albacore
tuna, drained

1 rib (stalk) celery, finely diced

2 tablespoons minced
fresh parsley

2 tablespoons sweet
green pickle relish

1 teaspoon fresh lemon juice

½ cup (4 oz/125 ml)
mayonnaise

4 thick slices sourdough bread

1 cup (4 oz/125 g) shredded
sharp Cheddar cheese

4 lemon wedges

4 sprigs fresh parsley

❖ Preheat a broiler (griller).

❖ In a bowl, combine the tuna, celery, parsley, pickle relish, lemon juice, and mayonnaise. Toss with a fork until well mixed.

❖ Place the bread slices on the broiler (griller) pan. Divide the tuna mixture evenly among them, mounding it slightly. Sprinkle the cheese evenly over the top.

❖ Place under the broiler and broil (grill) until the tops just begin to bubble and are golden, 3–4 minutes. Watch carefully or the cheese may brown too much.

❖ Transfer to individual plates and garnish with a lemon wedge and a parsley sprig. Serve immediately.

chicken noodle
vegetable soup

6 cups (48 fl oz/1.5 l)
chicken stock

1 yellow onion, finely chopped

2 carrots, peeled, halved
lengthwise, and thinly sliced

2 ribs (stalks) celery, thinly sliced

2 zucchini (courgettes),
thinly sliced

2 tablespoons finely
chopped fresh parsley

2 oz (60 g) dried very thin
egg noodles

½ cup (3 oz/90 g) shredded or
cubed skinless cooked
chicken meat

salt and ground black pepper

◈ In a large saucepan over medium–low heat, bring the chicken stock to a simmer. Add the onion, carrot, and celery and continue to simmer until the vegetables are slightly soft, about 10 minutes. Add the zucchini and 1 tablespoon of the parsley and cook until the zucchini is just tender, about 10 minutes longer.

◈ Add the noodles and simmer until just tender, 3–4 minutes, or according to the package directions.

◈ Three minutes before the noodles are done, add the chicken and heat through. Season with salt and pepper to taste.

◈ Ladle into warmed soup bowls and sprinkle the tops with the remaining 1 tablespoon parsley. Serve immediately.

reuben
sandwich

serves 4

A New York City restaurant called Reuben's first made this classic sandwich. If you like, substitute pastrami for the corned beef. Make sure to squeeze the sauerkraut quite dry to avoid a soggy sandwich. Serve with a side dish of onion rings or thin slices of dill pickles (pickled cucumbers).

8 slices rye bread with caraway seeds

¼ cup (2 oz/60 g) unsalted butter, at room temperature

¾ cup (6 fl oz/180 ml) Thousand Island dressing

4 oz (125 g) corned beef, thinly sliced

1 cup (6 oz/180 g) well-drained sauerkraut

2 cups (8 oz/250 g) Swiss cheese, shredded

✧ On a large work surface, lay out the bread slices. Spread one side of each slice evenly with the butter. Turn the slices over and spread the other side evenly with the dressing.

✧ Lay the sliced corned beef on the dressing-spread side of four of the bread slices, tucking in any overhang. Spread the sauerkraut evenly atop the corned beef, then distribute the cheese evenly over the sauerkraut. Top with the remaining bread slices, buttered side out, and press down firmly to compact the sandwiches.

✧ Heat a large nonstick frying pan or a griddle until hot. Working in batches if necessary and using a spatula, carefully transfer the sandwiches to the hot pan or griddle. Cook, pressing down gently on each sandwich with the spatula three or four times, until golden on the first side, 4–5 minutes. Carefully turn the sandwiches over and cook, again pressing down on them, until the second side is golden and the cheese has melted, 3–4 minutes longer. Turn over one more time and cook 2–3 minutes longer.

✧ Transfer to warmed individual plates and serve immediately.

roasted peppers
with melted cheese

serves 6

A classic northern Mexican dish, *queso fundido* (literally, "melted cheese") makes a delightful starter for a cold-weather meal. Serve with plenty of warm tortillas to scoop up the bubbling mixture. For more spice, add crunchy browned chunks of chorizo sausage or drizzle with chile salsa.

1 large, mild, fresh green chile (such as poblano or Anaheim), roasted, peeled, and seeded

1 each red and yellow bell pepper (capsicum), roasted, peeled, and seeded

1/2 white onion, diced

1 1/2 cups (6 oz/185 g) shredded Manchego, mozzarella, Monterey Jack, or other good melting cheese

1/2 cup (2 oz/60 g) grated Cotija or Romano cheese or crumbled feta cheese

1/2 cup (2 oz/60 g) crumbled panela, cottage, or ricotta cheese

ground black pepper

12 small flour or corn tortillas, homemade or purchased, heated

salsa of your choice, homemade (pages 28–29) or purchased

◈ Preheat oven to 375°F (190°C/Gas Mark 4). Cut the chile and bell peppers lengthwise into strips 3 inches (7.5 cm) long and ¼ inch (6 mm) wide. Place in a bowl, add the onion, and toss to mix. Set aside.

◈ In a separate bowl, combine all the cheeses; toss to mix. Set six 1-cup (8-fl oz/250-ml) or one 1½-qt (1.5-liter) earthenware or glass baking dish(es) in the oven to heat thoroughly, about 10 minutes.

◈ Distribute the cheeses evenly among the warmed small dishes or spread them evenly in the warmed large dish and return to the oven. Cook for 5 minutes. Sprinkle the cheeses with the pepper-onion mixture and return again to the oven. Bake until the cheeses are completely melted and beginning to bubble and turn golden, 5–7 minutes.

◈ Sprinkle with black pepper and serve immediately with warm tortillas and salsa on the side.

recipe **hint**

To roast chiles or bell peppers (capsicums), rub them lightly with oil (wear gloves when handling hot chiles), place in a baking tray, and roast in a preheated 400°F (200°C/Gas Mark 5) oven, turning from time to time, until charred on all sides. (Or, broil (grill), turning as needed, until all sides are blackened and blistered.) Place the hot chiles or bell peppers in a plastic bag, seal, and leave to sweat for 5–10 minutes (the steam created will help loosen the skin, making them easier to peel). Peel away the skin, removing any clinging skin with your fingertips or a small, sharp paring knife.

welsh rarebit

serves 4

SALAD

3 radishes, trimmed, sliced, and lightly salted

8 small pickled onions

¾ cup (¾ oz/20 g) lightly packed inner yellow frisée leaves

¾ cup (¾ oz/20 g) lightly packed arugula (rocket) leaves

RAREBIT

2 slices dense-textured white sandwich bread

2 slices dense-textured brown sandwich bread

1 cup (4 oz/125 g) shredded good-quality sharp Cheddar cheese

5 tablespoons (3 fl oz/80 ml) dark ale

2 tablespoons chilled unsalted butter, cut into pieces

1 tablespoon Dijon mustard

½ teaspoon salt, plus extra to taste

¼ teaspoon ground black pepper, plus extra to taste

pinch of cayenne pepper

❖ Preheat a broiler (griller). To make the salad, in a small bowl, toss together the radishes, pickled onions, frisée, and arugula.

❖ To make the rarebit, place the bread slices on a baking sheet. Place under the broiler and toast, turning once, until golden brown on both sides. Remove from the broiler.

❖ In a small saucepan over medium heat, combine the Cheddar and the dark ale. When the cheese melts, add the butter, Dijon mustard, ½ teaspoon salt, ¼ teaspoon pepper, and the cayenne pepper. Whisk together until evenly melted and combined.

❖ Cut each piece of toast in half diagonally and arrange on a flameproof platter or individual flameproof plates. Pour the cheese mixture over the toasts so they are covered completely. Place the platter or plates under the broiler and broil (grill) until the cheese bubbles and starts to scorch in places, about 2 minutes. Remove from the broiler.

❖ Serve immediately, with the salad on the side.

lemon-ginger shrimp

serves 8

3 lb (1.5 kg) uncooked jumbo shrimp (king prawns)

½ cup (4 fl oz/125 ml) olive oil

2 teaspoons toasted (Asian) sesame oil

¼ cup (2 fl oz/60 ml) lemon juice

1 onion, chopped

2 cloves garlic

2 tablespoons peeled and grated fresh ginger

2 tablespoons cilantro (fresh coriander) leaves

❖ Peel the shrimp, leaving tails intact, and devein.

❖ Pour the oils into the bowl of a food processor, add the lemon juice, onion, garlic, ginger, and cilantro, and process until puréed.

❖ Place the shrimp in a bowl, pour on the marinade, and let stand in the refrigerator for at least 2 hours.

❖ Preheat a broiler (griller). Thread the shrimp onto metal skewers, or bamboo skewers that have been soaked in water for at least 1 hour. Broil (grill), turning and basting frequently with the marinade, until the shrimp are just cooked, about 5 minutes. Serve at once.

smoked turkey pizza

1 large (9½-inch/24-cm) pita bread pocket, piece of lavash bread, or purchased pizza base

½ cup (4 fl oz/125 g) homemade or purchased tomato pasta sauce

3½ oz (100 g) smoked turkey, sliced

1 small onion, thinly sliced

1 tablespoon capers

1 tablespoon redcurrant or cranberry jelly, warmed

❖ Preheat oven to 450°F (230°C/Gas Mark 6).

❖ Place the bread or pizza base on a baking sheet. Spread the tomato sauce over the base and arrange the smoked turkey, onion, and capers over the pizza.

❖ Bake until the pizza is golden on the edges and crisp underneath, about 15 minutes. Brush with the redcurrant or cranberry jelly and serve immediately.

seafood gazpacho

4 tomatoes, peeled, seeded, and finely chopped

1 medium cucumber, peeled, seeded, and finely chopped

1 pimiento or small red bell pepper (capsicum), peeled, seeded, and finely chopped

1 small yellow bell pepper (capsicum), peeled, seeded, and finely chopped

1 red (Spanish) onion, finely chopped

2 cloves garlic, minced

dash of hot-pepper sauce, such as Tabasco

1 teaspoon ground cumin

juice of 1 lime

4 cups (32 fl oz/1 liter) tomato juice

2 tablespoons balsamic vinegar

½ cup (4 fl oz/125 ml) olive oil

salt and pepper

¼ cup (¼ oz/7 g) chopped cilantro (fresh coriander)

1 avocado, peeled, pitted, and finely chopped

1 cup (8 oz/250 g) chopped combined shrimp (prawn) and crab meat

cilantro (fresh coriander) leaves, to serve

Combine the tomato, cucumber, pimiento, bell pepper, and onion in a large bowl. Add the garlic, hot-pepper sauce, cumin, and lime juice. Add the tomato juice and balsamic vinegar and stir to combine. Stir in the oil. Season to taste with salt and pepper, add the chopped cilantro, and refrigerate until well chilled.

Just before serving, stir in the avocado and combined shrimp and crab meat. Sprinkle with the cilantro leaves and serve immediately.

recipe hint

Pimientos (from the Spanish for pepper) are sweet, heart-shaped, scarlet peppers about 4 inches (10 cm) long. They range in heat from mild to hot. Their thick flesh has more flavor than that of red bell peppers (capsicums), though if pimientos are unavailable, these may be substituted. Ground dried pimientos are better known as paprika, a spice essential to Hungarian and Spanish cuisine.

figs and prosciutto
with strawberry vinaigrette

makes 12

1½ cups (6 oz/185 g)
strawberries

2 tablespoons balsamic vinegar,
or to taste

½ cup (4 fl oz/125 ml) olive oil

6 slices prosciutto,
cut in half lengthwise

12 large figs

¼ cup (2 fl oz/60 ml) brandy

ground black pepper

❖ Preheat oven to 300°F (150°C/Gas Mark 2).

❖ For the vinaigrette, place the strawberries and vinegar in a blender container or food processor bowl. Blend or process until smooth. With the motor running, add the oil in a slow, steady stream through the hole in the lid of the blender container or the feed tube of the processor. Blend or process until combined, adding more vinegar if you prefer a sharper vinaigrette.

❖ Wrap a piece of prosciutto around each fig. Make a cross-shaped incision in the top of each fig and drizzle on a little brandy. Sprinkle with pepper and bake in the oven for 10 minutes. Serve warm, with a drizzle of strawberry vinaigrette.

pancetta
and pepperoni
pizza

serves 2–4

1 large (9½-inch/24-cm) pita
bread pocket, piece of
lavash bread, or purchased
pizza base

1 cup (8 fl oz/250 ml)
homemade or purchased
tomato pasta sauce

3½ oz (100 g) pepperoni,
thinly sliced

3½ oz (100 g) pancetta,
thinly sliced

½ cup (1¾ oz/50 g) shredded
mozzarella cheese

◇ Preheat oven to 450°F (230°C/Gas Mark 6).

◇ Place the bread or pizza base on a baking sheet.
Spread the tomato sauce over the surface. Arrange the
pepperoni, pancetta, and mozzarella over the top.

◇ Bake until the pizza is golden on the edges and
crisp underneath, about 15 minutes. Serve immediately.

chicken and walnut on rye

serves 3

¼ cup (2 oz/60 g) butter, at room temperature

1 tablespoon Dijon mustard

1 tablespoon chopped chives

6 slices rye bread

6 oz (185 g) Camembert cheese

1 avocado

1 tomato

6 large slices cooked chicken

¼ cup (2 fl oz/60 ml) mayonnaise

2 tablespoons sour cream

2 tablespoons chopped walnuts

◈ Combine the butter, mustard, and chives; spread onto one side of each slice of bread.

◈ Slice the cheese. Peel, pit, and slice the avocado. Slice the tomato.

◈ Arrange the chicken, Camembert, avocado, and tomato on the bread.

◈ Combine the mayonnaise, sour cream, and walnuts and spoon over the top of the filling. Serve at once.

egg scramble
with cheese, chives, and bacon

serves 4

3 slices (rashers) bacon

6 eggs

2 tablespoons finely chopped chives

1/2 teaspoon salt

1/4 teaspoon coarsely ground black pepper

1/4 cup (1 oz/30 g) shredded Cheddar cheese

4 slices whole wheat (wholemeal) or multi-grain bread, toasted and buttered

◈ Very finely shred the bacon. Heat a small frying pan and sauté the bacon until lightly crisped. Remove with a slotted spoon and drain on paper towels.

◈ Beat the eggs, adding half the chives, the salt and pepper, and most of the bacon, reserving a little for garnish. Stir in the cheese.

◈ Pour the bacon drippings into an omelet pan or nonstick frying pan and heat to moderate. Pour in the egg mixture and stir slowly until just set.

◈ Serve over buttered toast and garnish with the remaining chives and reserved bacon.

summer squash soup

¼ cup (2 oz/60 g) butter

10–12 (1 lb/500 g) small yellow summer (crookneck or straight) squash, peeled if desired and sliced

1 large onion, chopped

1 small clove garlic, minced

5 oz (150 g) broccoli, chopped

2–3 tablespoons all-purpose (plain) flour

1 cup (8 fl oz/250 ml) whole or skim milk

small pinch of fresh thyme

1 cup (8 fl oz/250 ml) chicken or vegetable stock

✧ Melt the butter in a large frying pan and sauté the squash, onion, and garlic until limp, about 10 minutes. Add the broccoli and cook until it is also soft and limp, about 10 minutes more.

✧ Mix in the flour, being careful not to let the mixture burn. When well combined and cooked slightly, remove from the heat and gradually add the milk and thyme, mixing well.

✧ Return to the heat and stir in the stock. Cook until the vegetables are soft and the soup is thickened, then reduce the heat to low and simmer for 5 minutes more.

✧ Serve at once. If desired, the soup may be frozen for up to 2 months. To serve, thaw in the refrigerator and heat gently, stirring occasionally, or thaw and heat in a microwave oven.

quick pita bread pizza

serves 2–4

2 large (8-inch/20-cm) white pita bread pockets

¼ cup (2 fl oz/60 ml) homemade or purchased tomato pasta sauce

6 thick slices spicy salami, shredded

2 thick slices cooked ham, finely diced or ground (minced)

2 tablespoons sliced stuffed green olives

3 tablespoons diced green bell pepper (capsicum)

3 tablespoons drained and crushed or finely diced canned pineapple

2 teaspoons dried Italian or Provençal mixed herbs

½ cup (2 oz/60 g) shredded mozzarella or other melting cheese

◈ Place the pita breads on a baking sheet and spread with the pasta sauce.

◈ Combine the salami and ham and spread evenly over the pita breads.

◈ Top with the remaining ingredients, scattering the cheese on top.

◈ Heat under a hot broiler (griller) until the cheese melts, about 4 minutes.

◈ Serve immediately.

delicious dips

tapenade

1½ cups (7 oz/220 g) pitted black olives in brine, such as Niçoise or Kalamata, patted dry

2 drained, oil-packed anchovy fillets

¼ cup (2 oz/60 g) canned oil-packed tuna, drained (optional)

3 tablespoons capers

1 clove garlic, finely chopped

3 tablespoons extra-virgin olive oil

✥ Place the olives in the bowl of a food processor and purée until roughly chopped. Add anchovies, tuna (if using), capers, garlic, and oil. Process for 30 seconds.

✥ Store in an airtight container in the refrigerator for up to 1 week.

makes 1½ cups (12 oz/375 g)

taramasalata

1 cup (8 oz/250 g) tarama (carp roe), red or golden whitefish caviar, or smoked cod roe

1 cup (8 oz/250 g) cream cheese, at room temperature

1 small clove garlic, chopped

1 tablespoon lemon juice

ground black pepper

2 tablespoons olive oil

1 tablespoon heavy (double) cream

✥ In a food processor, process the tarama, cream cheese, garlic, lemon juice, and pepper to taste until combined. With the motor running, add the olive oil and cream and process until smooth.

✥ Store in an airtight container in the refrigerator for 2–3 days.

makes 1½ cups (12 oz/375 g)

guacamole

3 ripe avocados

1 fresh green chile, stemmed, seeded, and finely chopped

1/2 white onion, diced

1/3 cup (1/3 oz/10 g) coarsely chopped fresh cilantro (fresh coriander)

juice of 1 lime

1/2 teaspoon salt

ground black pepper

pinch of cayenne pepper (optional)

corn tortilla chips

✧ Cut each avocado lengthwise into quarters and remove the pit. Peel off the skin and place the pulp in a bowl. Using a fork, mash lightly.

✧ Add the remaining ingredients and mix just until combined; chunks of avocado should remain visible.

✧ Serve immediately accompanied with tortilla chips.

makes about 2 cups (16 oz/500 g)

crab dip

1/4 cup (2 oz/60 g) cream cheese, at room temperature

1 tablespoon mayonnaise

1/3 cup (2 oz/60 g) each finely chopped red and green bell pepper (capsicum)

2 tablespoons finely chopped yellow bell pepper (capsicum)

2 green (spring) onions, finely chopped

1 clove garlic, finely chopped

1 tablespoon lemon juice

dash of hot-pepper sauce, such as Tabasco

salt and pepper

1/2 cup (4 oz/125 g) crabmeat, drained

1 tablespoon chopped fresh dill

✧ Combine cream cheese, mayonnaise, bell pepper, green onion, and garlic. Stir to combine. Add lemon juice, hot-pepper sauce, and salt and pepper to taste. Mix well. Stir in crabmeat and dill. Allow to stand for 1 hour before serving.

makes 2 cups (16 oz/500 g)

sautéed chicken sandwich

serves 4

¼ cup (1½ oz/45 g) chopped pimiento-
stuffed olives or Kalamata olives

1 small tomato, chopped

1 tablespoon chopped fresh parsley

2 teaspoons drained capers (optional)

½ teaspoon dried Italian seasoning,
crushed

1 teaspoon olive oil or vegetable oil,
plus 2 tablespoons extra

4 boneless, skinless chicken breast
halves (about 1 lb/500g total)

4 lettuce leaves

4 slices sourdough bread, toasted

❖ In a small mixing bowl, combine the olives, tomato, parsley, capers (if using), Italian seasoning, and the 1 teaspoon oil. Set aside.

❖ Place each breast half between 2 pieces of plastic wrap. Working from the center to the edges, pound chicken lightly with the flat side of a meat mallet to a ¼-inch (5-mm) thickness. Remove plastic wrap.

❖ In a large frying pan over medium–high heat, warm the 2 tablespoons oil. Add the chicken and cook, turning once, until tender and no pink remains, 4–6 minutes total.

❖ To serve, place the lettuce leaves on the toasted sourdough bread. Top with the chicken breasts and olive mixture.

marinara pizza

serves 2–4

1 large (9½-inch/24-cm) pita bread
pocket, piece of lavash bread, or
purchased pizza base

½ cup (4 fl oz/125 ml) homemade or
purchased tomato pasta sauce

8 oz (250 g) assorted prepared seafood
of your choice, such as large uncooked
shrimp (prawns), shelled mussels,
calamari rings, fish pieces,
baby octopus, or shelled scallops

¼ cup (1 oz/30g) shredded
mozzarella cheese

✥ Preheat oven to 450°F (230°C/Gas Mark 6).

✥ Place the bread or pizza base on a baking
sheet and spread with the tomato sauce.
Arrange the seafood over the top and then
sprinkle with the mozzarella cheese.

✥ Bake until the pizza is golden on the edges
and the seafood is just cooked through,
15–20 minutes. Serve at once.

bruschetta

with tomatoes, beans, and fresh herbs

serves 4

TOPPING

1 large ripe tomato, seeded and diced

¾ cup (5½ oz/170 g) well-drained cannellini beans (home cooked or canned)

¼ cup (1¼ oz/35 g) seeded and diced cucumber

2 tablespoons thinly sliced green (spring) onion

1 tablespoon fresh oregano leaves or 1½ teaspoons dried oregano

1 tablespoon chopped fresh basil or 1½ teaspoons dried basil

ground black pepper

BRUSCHETTA

8 slices country-style white or whole wheat (wholemeal) bread, each 2½ inches (6 cm) wide and ½ inch (10 mm) thick

1 large clove garlic, halved

4 teaspoons extra-virgin olive oil

To make the topping, combine all the topping ingredients in a bowl, adding pepper to taste. Toss well, cover, and refrigerate for at least 1–2 hours or for up to 2 days to allow the flavors to blend.

To make the bruschetta, preheat a broiler (griller). Arrange the bread slices on a rack on a broiler pan and broil (grill) for 2 minutes. Turn the bread slices and continue to cook until golden, 1–2 minutes longer. Remove from the heat, rub a cut side of the garlic clove over one side of each piece of warm toast, and then brush with ½ teaspoon of the olive oil.

Mound an equal amount of the topping on the garlic-rubbed side of each piece of toast. Transfer to a warmed platter and serve immediately.

Bruschetta, a classic Italian appetizer, was originally devised as a way of using up leftover bread. In its most basic form, it is simply toasted bread rubbed with garlic and drizzled with olive oil. In Tuscany, where olive oil is almost sacred, this dish is called *fettunta* (literally an "anointed" slice of bread). The addition of chopped tomatoes, and a few anchovy fillets if desired, turns it into a delicious light lunch. Other toppings for bruschetta include sliced bocconcini with basil leaves, tapenade (page 68), or salsas (pages 28–29).

clams
in white wine

serves 4

2 lb (1 kg) small clams

salt

1/3 cup (3 fl oz/90 ml) olive oil

2 cloves garlic, finely chopped

2 teaspoons dry bread crumbs

1/3 cup (3 fl oz/90 ml) water

1/3 cup (3 fl oz/90 ml)
dry white wine

2 teaspoons chopped parsley

❖ Soak the clams in salted water for 3–4 hours to release any sand, shaking them around occasionally. Discard any clams that do not sink to the bottom.

❖ Warm the oil in a heatproof casserole over medium heat and sauté the garlic until lightly colored, about 5 minutes. Add the clams and sauté on low heat until they open. Mix the bread crumbs with the water and add to the casserole along with the white wine.

❖ Cook over low heat for 10 minutes, gently shaking the casserole occasionally to thicken the sauce.

❖ Sprinkle with the parsley and serve very hot.

stracciatella alla fiorentina

serves 4–6

6 cups (48 fl oz/1.5 l)
chicken stock

2 oz (60 g) stemmed fresh
spinach leaves

4 eggs

¼ cup (1 oz/30 g) grated
Parmesan cheese

◈ In a large saucepan, bring the stock to a boil, then reduce to a brisk simmer.

◈ Meanwhile, take half of the spinach leaves, stack them, roll them tightly lengthwise into a cylinder, and slice crosswise into thin shreds. Repeat with the remaining leaves.

◈ In a bowl, lightly beat the eggs, then stir in the cheese. While stirring the stock constantly, drizzle in the egg mixture, then add the spinach.

◈ Simmer for 2–3 minutes more, then serve at once.

quick and easy
pasta

sun-dried tomato pasta

serves 3–4

1 tablespoon olive oil

1 small onion, finely chopped

1 medium carrot, finely chopped

1 rib (stick) celery, finely chopped

1 clove garlic, crushed

2 cans (each 14 oz/400 g) chopped tomatoes

4 oz (125 g) drained, chopped, oil-packed,
sun-dried tomatoes

²/₃ cup (5 fl oz/150 ml) light stock

½ cup (4 fl oz/125 ml) dry white wine

salt and ground black pepper

8 oz (250 g) dried fettuccine, tagliatelle,
or spaghetti

shaved or grated Parmesan cheese, to serve

In a large pan over medium heat, warm the oil. Add the onion, carrot, celery, and garlic and cook, stirring, until the vegetables soften, about 5 minutes. Stir in the tomatoes, stock, wine, and salt and pepper to taste. Cover and simmer for about 20 minutes, stirring occasionally.

Meanwhile, cook the pasta in boiling salted water until tender.

Blend half the sauce in a food processor, then return it to the pan, stirring it into the remaining sauce.

Drain the cooked pasta and top with the sauce and Parmesan cheese.

tomato pasta with mozzarella

serves 3–4

8 oz (250 g) dried pasta
of any kind

1 lb (500 g) ripe tomatoes

grated zest of 1 lemon

3 tablespoons balsamic vinegar

salt and ground black pepper

1 tablespoon olive oil

1 tablespoon
chopped fresh thyme

8 oz (250 g) mozzarella
cheese, diced

❖ Cook the pasta in boiling salted water until tender.

❖ Meanwhile, seed and finely chop the tomatoes. Place in a medium saucepan with the lemon zest, vinegar, and salt and pepper to taste. Warm the tomato mixture over low heat for 2–3 minutes.

❖ When the pasta is cooked, drain and transfer to a large serving bowl. Add the olive oil and thyme and toss well. Spoon the sauce over the pasta, top with the mozzarella, and serve immediately.

pasta with
chile pesto

1 large red bell pepper (capsicum)

2 cups (2 oz/60 g) fresh basil

1 clove garlic, crushed

2 ripe tomatoes, peeled

2 tablespoons pine nuts

3 tablespoons sun-dried tomato paste

3 tablespoons tomato purée

1 tablespoon mild chili powder

few drops of hot-pepper sauce

½ cup (2 oz/60 g) grated Parmesan cheese

⅔ cup (5 fl oz/150 ml) olive oil

1 lb (500 g) dried ribbon pasta

❖ Grill (broil) the bell pepper, turning occasionally, until evenly charred all over. Place in a plastic bag, seal, and allow to sweat for 5–10 minutes.

❖ Meanwhile, cook the pasta in boiling salted water until tender.

❖ Peel, halve, and seed the bell pepper. Place the flesh in the bowl of a food processor along with the basil, garlic, tomato, pine nuts, tomato paste, tomato purée, chili powder, hot-pepper sauce, and Parmesan cheese. Process until almost smooth. Stir in the oil.

❖ Drain the cooked pasta, keeping back 2 tablespoons of water in the pan. Return the pasta to the pan and add the chile pesto, allowing about 2 tablespoons per person. Toss to combine and serve immediately.

serves 4–6

*6½ oz (200 g) smoked
salmon*

*1 cup (8 fl oz/250 ml) heavy
(double) cream*

1 tablespoon chopped chives

1 tablespoon chopped dill

1 lb (500 g) fresh linguine

*whipped cream,
salmon caviar, chopped
chives, and dill sprigs,
to garnish (optional)*

❖ Cut half of the salmon into thin strips. Set aside.

❖ Roughly chop the remaining salmon. In the bowl of a food processor, combine the chopped salmon and the cream. Process just long enough to make the mixture smooth; avoid whipping the cream. Pour the cream mixture into a saucepan, add the chives and dill, and warm gently while you cook the pasta. (Do not allow the sauce to boil.)

❖ Cook the pasta in boiling salted water until al dente. Drain and place in a large, warmed serving bowl. Add the cream sauce and the sliced salmon and toss through. Garnish with cream, salmon caviar, chives, and dill, if desired.

linguine
with smoked salmon
and herb sauce

individual
tortellini salads

1 lb (500 g) purchased tortellini filled with ham and ricotta

DRESSING

½ cup (4 fl oz/125 ml) extra-virgin olive oil

2 tablespoons balsamic vinegar

1 small clove garlic, crushed

salt and ground black pepper

SALAD

6½ oz (200 g) cherry tomatoes, halved

3½ oz (100 g) tiny black olives

1 bunch arugula (rocket), washed and dried

1 cup (1 oz/30 g) shredded basil leaves

6½ oz (200 g) spicy salami, cut into thin strips

2 small red (Spanish) onions, cut into thin rings

10 drained, oil-packed, sun-dried tomatoes, cut into strips

½ cup (1¾ oz/50 g) Parmesan shavings

❖ Cook the tortellini in a large amount of boiling salted water until tender, 10–15 minutes or as directed on the package.

❖ Combine all the dressing ingredients in a screwtop jar and shake vigorously.

❖ While the pasta is cooking, prepare all the other ingredients.

❖ Drain the tortellini thoroughly and place in a shallow baking dish. Pour on two-thirds of the dressing and gently toss to coat each piece thoroughly. Allow the tortellini to cool to room temperature, then toss the pasta with the remaining salad ingredients.

❖ When ready to serve, pile the salad onto serving plates, top with the Parmesan shavings, and drizzle on a little more of the dressing.

filipino-style noodles

serves 4

2 tablespoons vegetable oil

½ cup (2 oz/60 g)
chopped onion

2 cloves garlic, minced

1 cup (4 oz/125 g) thinly
bias-sliced carrots

1 small zucchini (courgette),
thinly sliced

1 cup (3 oz/90 g) shredded
cabbage

1 cup (8 fl oz/250 ml)
chicken stock, or as needed

2 tablespoons soy sauce

5 oz (155 g) cooked
pork, sliced

5 oz (155 g) cooked peeled
prawns, chopped

8 oz (250 g) dried Chinese
egg noodles

1 oz (30 g) sliced green
(spring) onions (optional)

❖ In a large frying pan, warm the oil. When hot, add the onion and garlic and cook, stirring, until tender but not brown, about 5 minutes. Add the carrot, zucchini, cabbage, stock, and soy sauce; mix well. Bring to a boil, then reduce the heat, cover, and simmer for 5 minutes, or until the carrot is crisp-tender. Stir in the pork and prawns.

❖ Break the noodles apart and stir into the cooked mixture. (If necessary, add a little extra chicken stock to cook the noodles.) Cover and cook over low heat until the noodles are tender and the liquid is absorbed, 4–6 minutes. Stir the mixture gently and transfer to a serving dish. If desired, sprinkle with green onions.

summer
spaghetti

serves 4–6

1 lb (500 g) firm ripe tomatoes,
peeled, seeded, and finely chopped

1 red (Spanish) onion, diced

1 small red chile, stemmed, seeded,
and minced

12 stuffed green olives, finely chopped

1 tablespoon capers,
chopped if large

1½ teaspoons finely chopped
fresh oregano

⅓ cup (⅓ oz/10 g) finely
chopped parsley

2 cloves garlic, crushed

½ cup (4 fl oz/125 ml)
extra-virgin olive oil

3–4 slices prosciutto

1 lb (500 g) spaghetti

❖ Combine all of the
ingredients except the
prosciutto and pasta in a
bowl. Mix well; cover and
let stand overnight.

❖ Cook the pasta in boiling
salted water until al dente.
Meanwhile, in a small frying
pan, cook the prosciutto until
crisp. Crumble.

❖ Serve the pasta sauce at
room temperature over the
hot pasta, topped with the
crumbled prosciutto.

penne
with mushrooms
and tarragon

1 lb (500 g) dried penne

¼ cup (2 oz/60 g) butter

8 oz (250 g) small white
(button) mushrooms,
thickly sliced

1 clove garlic, crushed

2 teaspoons fresh tarragon,
finely chopped

salt and ground black pepper

1¼ cups (10 fl oz/300 ml)
heavy (whipping) cream

1 teaspoon grated
lemon zest

½ cup (2 oz/60 g) freshly
grated Parmesan cheese

❖ Cook the pasta in plenty of boiling salted water until al dente.

❖ Meanwhile, melt the butter in a frying pan. Add the mushrooms and sauté gently for about 1 minute. Add the garlic and cook for 30 seconds. Add the tarragon, salt and pepper to taste, cream, and lemon zest. Stir over low heat for 2 minutes. Add the Parmesan cheese and cook gently until the mixture thickens slightly, about 3 minutes.

❖ Drain the pasta and stir it into the hot sauce. Serve immediately.

spaghetti
with pesto, shallots, and olives

serves 3–4

1 tablespoon butter

2 tablespoons olive oil

8 oz (250 g) golden (French) shallots or small yellow onions, thinly sliced

8 oz (250 g) dried spaghetti

2 oz (60 g) pitted black olives

2 tablespoons (1 fl oz/30 ml) basil pesto

salt and ground black pepper

chopped fresh basil, to garnish

❖ Warm the butter and oil in a frying pan over low–medium heat. Add the shallot or onion and cook gently, stirring occasionally, until soft and golden, 10–15 minutes.

❖ Meanwhile, cook the pasta in boiling salted water until tender.

❖ Stir the olives and pesto into the onion mixture, warm through, and add salt and pepper to taste.

❖ Drain the cooked pasta and return it to the pan. Add the sauce and toss well. Serve immediately, garnished with basil.

three-cheese macaroni

serves 4–6

8 oz (250 g) macaroni

2 oz (60 g) butter

1½ oz (45 g) all-purpose (plain) flour

1 bay leaf

3½ cups (875 ml) milk, preferably low-fat (semi-skimmed)

8 oz (250 g) Fontina, Gouda, or Edam cheese, coarsely shredded

2 teaspoons Dijon mustard

salt and ground black pepper

pinch of grated nutmeg

4 oz (125 g) mozzarella cheese, roughly chopped

2 oz (60 g) grated Parmesan cheese

½ oz (15 g) fresh white bread crumbs

parsley, to garnish

✧ Cook the pasta in boiling salted water until tender. Drain and set aside.

✧ Meanwhile, in a medium saucepan, melt the butter, then stir in the flour and bay leaf. Cook, stirring, for 1–2 minutes, then gradually stir in the milk. Bring to the boil, stirring constantly until slightly thickened. Remove the bay leaf.

✧ Remove from the heat and beat in the cheese, mustard, salt and pepper to taste, and the nutmeg. Fold in the macaroni, mozzarella, and half of the Parmesan. Return to the heat and stir until piping hot. Spoon into a greased, shallow 1½-qt (1.5-liter) ovenproof casserole. Sprinkle with the remaining Parmesan and the bread crumbs. Place under a hot broiler (griller) until just browned. Serve garnished with parsley.

cappelletti
with mushrooms

serves 4

1 oz (30 g) dried porcini
mushrooms

10 fl oz (300 ml) warm water

8 oz (250 g) cappelletti or
other dried pasta shapes

2 tablespoons butter

1 onion, finely chopped

1 clove garlic, crushed

8 oz (250 g) button
mushrooms, sliced

salt and ground black pepper

1 tablespoon
chopped fresh chives

❖ Soak the porcini in the warm water for about
20 minutes. Drain, reserving the soaking liquid, and
slice the mushrooms.

❖ Meanwhile, cook the pasta in boiling salted water
until tender.

❖ Melt the butter in a frying pan, add the onion
and garlic, and sauté over low–medium heat until
softened. Add the dried and fresh mushrooms and
sauté for 3–4 minutes. Add the soaking liquid, increase
the heat to medium–high, and boil gently until reduced
by half, 4–5 minutes. Add salt and pepper to taste.

❖ Drain the cooked pasta and return it to the pan.
Add the sauce and chives, toss well, and serve at once.

pasta with mushrooms, thyme, and zucchini

serves 6

1 lb (500g) dried curly pasta shapes, such as spiralli, or shells

2 oz (60 g) butter

1 clove garlic, chopped

4–6 large flat mushrooms, sliced

1 tablespoon chopped fresh thyme

4 small zucchini (courgettes), coarsely shredded

salt and ground black pepper

shaved or grated pecorino or Parmesan cheese, to serve

✧ Cook the pasta in boiling salted water until tender.

✧ Meanwhile, melt the butter over low heat, add the garlic, and sauté until golden, 2–3 minutes.

✧ Add the mushrooms and fry over medium heat until softened and beginning to brown, about 2 minutes. Stir in the thyme and zucchini. Increase the heat and cook, stirring constantly, until the zucchini is tender. about 5 minutes. Add salt and pepper to taste.

✧ Drain the cooked pasta, keeping back 2 tablespoons of water in the pan. Return the pasta to the pan, add the sauce, and toss well. Serve immediately, topped with the pecorino or Parmesan.

spring vegetable pasta

serves 4

12 oz (375 g) dried penne

4 oz (125 g) fresh asparagus or French beans, trimmed and cut into 2-inch (5-cm) lengths

8 oz (250 g) thinly sliced small young leeks

6 oz (180 g) creamy goats' cheese, or full-fat soft cheese with garlic and herbs

5 oz (150 g) mascarpone cheese, or 5 fl oz (150 ml) extra-thick heavy (double) cream, plus extra to serve (optional)

2 oz (60 g) butter

2 tablespoons olive oil

4 oz (125 g) finely chopped onion

4 oz (125 g) finely sliced carrot

8 oz (250 g) brown-cap mushrooms (such as cremino, Portobello, or Swiss brown), thinly sliced

½ cup (4 fl oz/125 ml) dry white wine

1½ cups (12 oz/375 g) crème fraîche

¼ cup (¼ oz/7 g) chopped fresh herbs, such as parsley, thyme, or sage

4 oz (125 g) fresh baby peas

salt and ground black pepper

⬥ Cook the pasta in boiling salted water until tender.

⬥ Meanwhile, briefly blanch the asparagus or beans and leeks in boiling salted water for 3–4 minutes. Drain.

⬥ Combine the goats' cheese or soft cheese with the mascarpone or cream.

⬥ In a large frying pan, melt the butter with the oil. Add the onion and cook, stirring, for 3–4 minutes. Add the carrot and mushroom and continue to cook until beginning to soften, a further 2–3 minutes.

⬥ Stir in the wine, crème fraîche, herbs, peas, and blanched vegetables. Simmer gently until the sauce is thick enough to coat the vegetables well.

⬥ Remove the sauce from the heat and gently stir in the cheese mixture until thoroughly combined. Add salt and pepper to taste.

⬥ Drain the cooked pasta and transfer to a serving dish. Spoon the sauce over and serve immediately, garnished with extra mascarpone or cream, if desired.

seafood spaghetti

serves 4–6

2 lb (1 kg) mussels in their shells, scrubbed

9 oz (270 g) uncooked large shrimp (prawns)

1 lb (500 g) dried spaghetti

2 tablespoons butter

1/3 cup (3 fl oz/90 ml) white wine

1/4 cup (2 fl oz/60 ml) water

1 teaspoon grated lemon zest

2 teaspoons mild curry paste

1 1/4 cups (10 fl oz/300 ml) light (single) cream

6 oz (180 g) smoked salmon, sliced

salt and ground black pepper

❖ Discard any damaged mussels or open ones that do not close when tapped sharply. Peel and devein the prawns, then halve lengthwise.

❖ Cook the pasta in boiling salted water until tender.

❖ Meanwhile, combine the butter, wine, water, and mussels in a large pan. Cover tightly and cook briskly, shaking the pan occasionally, until the mussels open, about 4 minutes. Remove with a slotted spoon. Discard any that do not open. Remove mussel meat from shells.

❖ Add the shrimp to the same pan. Cook, stirring, until pink, 4–5 minutes. Add the lemon zest, curry paste, cream, smoked salmon, and mussel meat. Heat gently, adding salt and pepper to taste.

❖ Drain the cooked pasta and return it to the pan. Add the sauce, toss well, and serve at once.

spaghetti
with leeks and pancetta

serves 4–6

1 lb (500 g) dried spaghetti

2 tablespoons olive oil

2 medium leeks, thinly sliced

6 oz (180 g) pancetta, thinly sliced

1/3 cup (3 fl oz/90 ml) white wine

1 1/4 cups (10 fl oz/300 ml) light (single) cream

3 tablespoons grated Parmesan cheese

◈ Cook the pasta in boiling salted water until tender.

◈ Meanwhile, warm the oil in a frying pan over medium heat, add the leeks, and cook gently until softened, 3–4 minutes. Add the pancetta and cook until beginning to brown, 4–5 minutes more.

◈ Add the wine, stir to deglaze the pan, and bring nearly to the boil. Reduce the heat, add the cream, and warm through; do not allow to boil.

◈ Drain the cooked pasta and return to the pan. Add the sauce and Parmesan, toss well, and serve at once.

walnut and olive spaghetti

serves 4–6

1 lb (500 g) dried
whole wheat (wholemeal)
spaghetti

7½-oz (230-g) jar mixed olives
in extra-virgin olive oil

2½ oz (75 g) walnuts

juice of ½ orange
(3–4 tablespoons)

salt and ground black pepper

grated Parmesan cheese,
to serve

❖ Cook the pasta in boiling salted water until tender.

❖ Meanwhile, drain the olives, reserving the oil. Pit and slice the olives. Grate the walnuts, using a mouli grater or food processor, or chop them very finely.

❖ For the dressing, mix together the orange juice and reserved olive oil.

❖ Drain the cooked pasta, return it to the pan, and add the olives, walnuts, dressing, and salt and pepper to taste. Toss lightly to combine.

❖ Serve at once, topped with the Parmesan.

pasta mediterranean

1 lb (500 g) dried pasta shapes,
such as ballerine, radiatore,
farfalle, or cappelletti

6 oz (180 g) soft fresh
goats' cheese

2 tablespoons capers in vinegar,
drained

8 oz (250 g) mixed green and
black olives, pitted and
chopped

8 oil-packed sun-dried
tomatoes, drained and chopped

1 teaspoon dried oregano

salt and ground black pepper

❖ Cook the pasta in boiling salted water until tender.

❖ Meanwhile, combine the goats' cheese, capers, olives, sun-dried tomatoes, oregano, and salt and pepper to taste.

❖ Drain the cooked pasta, keeping back 2 tablespoons water in the pan. Return the pasta to the pan, add the sauce, and toss to combine. Cover and leave to stand for 3 minutes before serving.

cherry tomato and basil pasta

serves 4–6

1 lb (500 g) ripe cherry tomatoes, quartered

2 cloves garlic, finely chopped

1/4 cup (1/4 oz/7 g) shredded fresh basil

2/3 cup (5 fl oz/150 ml) extra-virgin olive oil

salt and ground black pepper

1 lb (500 g) dried chunky pasta shapes, such as rigatoni, penne, or farfalle

4 oz (125 g) feta cheese, thinly sliced

❖ In a bowl, combine the tomatoes, garlic, basil, olive oil, and salt and pepper to taste. Cover and leave to infuse at room temperature for at least 30 minutes; do not refrigerate.

❖ Cook the pasta in boiling salted water until tender. Drain, keeping back 2 tablespoons water in the pan. Return the pasta to the pan, add the sauce, and toss to combine. Remove from the heat, cover, and leave to stand for 3 minutes.

❖ Remove the lid, stir, and divide among serving bowls. Serve topped with slices of feta cheese.

garlic and anchovy pasta

serves 4–6

3 tablespoons olive oil

3 cloves garlic, chopped

1 small can oil-packed
anchovies, drained
and chopped

1 can (13 oz/400 g) chopped
tomatoes

ground black pepper

1 lb (500 g) dried farfalle,
bucatini, macaroni, or other
small pasta shapes

10 large fresh basil leaves,
shredded

4 oz (125 g) arugula (fresh
rocket) leaves

◈ Warm the olive oil in a saucepan over low–medium heat, add the garlic, and fry until just beginning to color, 2–3 minutes. Stir in the anchovies and cook gently until they begin to dissolve.

◈ Add the chopped tomatoes and bring to the boil. Add pepper to taste (salt won't be needed, because the anchovies are quite salty). Cover and simmer gently for 10 minutes.

◈ Meanwhile, cook the pasta in boiling salted water until tender. Drain, keeping back 2 tablespoons water in the pan. Reduce the heat to low and return the pasta to the pan.

◈ Stir the shredded basil into the sauce. Immediately add the sauce to the pasta and toss well. Serve each portion topped with a tangle of arugula leaves.

ricotta and spinach gnocchi

serves 4

1 tablespoon butter

½ cup (2½ oz/65 g) all-purpose (plain) flour

2 cups (16 fl oz/500 ml) skimmed milk

⅓ cup (3 oz/90 g) grated Parmesan cheese

14 oz (400 g) fresh spinach, wilted over low heat, well drained, and chopped, or 8 oz (250 g) frozen chopped spinach, thawed, well drained, and warmed through

5 oz (150 g) ricotta cheese

1 egg yolk

salt and ground black pepper

grated nutmeg

❖ Melt the butter in a saucepan, stir in ½ oz (15 g) of the flour, and cook over low heat for 1 minute. Remove the pan from the heat and gradually stir in the milk. Return to medium heat, bring to the boil, stirring, and cook until the sauce thickens. Simmer for 1–2 minutes more, then stir in 1 oz (30 g) Parmesan. Keep warm.

❖ Combine the well-drained, warmed spinach with the ricotta, the remaining 2 oz (50 g) flour, the egg yolk, and half of the remaining Parmesan. Add salt, pepper, and nutmeg to taste. Beat well.

❖ With floured hands, shape mixture into walnut-sized balls. Drop into simmering salted water and cook until the gnocchi float to the surface, 3–4 minutes. Drain and place in a greased flameproof dish. Spoon the sauce over the gnocchi and sprinkle with the remaining Parmesan. Grill (broil) until golden. Serve immediately.

pasta with bacon and wilted spinach

1 lb (500 g) dried spaghetti,
tagliatelle, or linguine

4 tablespoons olive oil

8 slices pancetta or unsmoked
bacon, chopped

2 cloves garlic, finely chopped

2 lb (1 kg) spinach leaves,
stalks removed

⅔ cup (5 fl oz/150 ml) heavy
(double) cream

salt and ground black pepper

grated nutmeg

3 tablespoons pine nuts,
toasted

❖ Cook the pasta in boiling salted water until tender.

❖ Meanwhile, warm the oil in a large frying pan over medium heat, add the pancetta or bacon, and fry until just turning golden, 4–5 minutes. Add the garlic and cook for 1 minute more.

❖ Stir in the spinach and cook over high heat for a few minutes or until the leaves are just wilted. Pour in the cream, turning the spinach to ensure it is well coated. Season with salt, pepper, and nutmeg to taste. Heat until simmering; do not allow to boil.

❖ Drain the pasta, keeping back 2 tablespoons water in the pan. Return the pasta to the pan, add the sauce, and toss well. Serve sprinkled with the pine nuts.

fettuccine
with asparagus

serves 4–6

1 lb (500 g) dried fettuccine

1/4 teaspoon saffron threads

5 oz (150 g) pancetta, diced

1 lb (500 g) fresh asparagus

1/3 cup (3 oz/90 g) butter

4 green (spring) onions, sliced

1/2 cup (4 fl oz/125 ml) white wine

1 cup (8 fl oz/250 ml) heavy (double) cream

3 tablespoons chopped fresh chives

2 oz (60 g) grated Parmesan cheese

salt and ground black pepper

◈ Cook the pasta in boiling salted water until tender.

◈ Soak the saffron in 2 tablespoons hot water.

◈ Preheat a heavy-based frying pan. Add the pancetta and fry, stirring, until golden and crisp. Set aside.

◈ Cut the asparagus into short lengths, keeping the tips whole. Parboil for 2 minutes; drain.

◈ Meanwhile, melt the butter in a large frying pan. Add the green onions and cook for 1 minute, then add the asparagus and sauté for 1–2 minutes. Add the wine and cook for 3 minutes. Stir in the cream, saffron, and its soaking liquid. Bring to a simmer.

◈ Drain the pasta, return it to the pan, and add the sauce, chives, Parmesan, pancetta, and salt and pepper to taste. Toss well and serve at once.

walnut and gorgonzola *pasta*

pasta

serves 4–6

2 slices whole wheat (wholemeal) bread, crusts removed

¾ cup (6 fl oz/180 ml) milk

8 oz (250 g) walnut pieces

1 lb (500 g) dried ribbon pasta, such pappardelle or fettuccine

1 clove garlic, crushed

4 oz (125 g) Gorgonzola cheese, chopped

¼ cup (2 fl oz/60 ml) extra-virgin olive oil

⅓ cup (3 fl oz/90 ml) crème fraîche

½ cup (½ oz/15 g) chopped fresh parsley

salt and ground black pepper

◈ Preheat oven to 375°F (190°C/Gas Mark 4). Soak the bread in the milk until all the milk is absorbed, about 10 minutes.

◈ Spread the walnuts on a baking sheet and toast in the oven for 5 minutes, shaking the baking sheet occasionally. Transfer to a plate and allow to cool.

◈ Meanwhile, cook the pasta in boiling salted water until tender.

◈ Place the soaked bread, walnuts, garlic, gorgonzola, and oil in the bowl of a food processor and process until almost smooth. Transfer to a bowl and stir in the crème fraîche and parsley. Add salt and pepper to taste.

◈ Drain the cooked pasta and return to the pan. Add the sauce and toss well. Remove from heat, cover with a lid, and leave to stand for 3 minutes before serving.

seared salmon
with saffron salsa

serves 4

SALSA

¼ teaspoon saffron threads

3 tomatoes, peeled, seeded, and diced

3 green (spring) onions, finely chopped

1 clove garlic, crushed

1 tablespoon shredded fresh basil

salt and ground black pepper

8 oz (250 g) dried fusilli, farfalle, or other pasta shapes

2 tablespoons extra-virgin olive oil, plus extra for brushing

2 teaspoons fresh thyme leaves

1 tablespoon lemon juice

1 tablespoon cracked black pepper

1 teaspoon cumin seeds

4 small skinless salmon fillets, each about 3 oz (90 g)

basil leaves, to garnish

✧ For the salsa, soak the saffron in 1 tablespoon boiling water for 10 minutes, then mix with the other salsa ingredients; set aside.

✧ Cook the pasta in boiling salted water until tender.

✧ Meanwhile, in a small saucepan, combine the oil, thyme, and lemon juice. Warm through over low heat.

✧ Drain the cooked pasta thoroughly and transfer to a large bowl. Add the oil mixture and toss well. Allow to cool.

✧ Preheat a ridged griddle or heavy-based frying pan over high heat until very hot. Combine the cracked pepper and cumin seeds and press firmly onto the salmon fillets. Brush the fillets with a little oil.

✧ Add the salmon to the griddle or frying pan and sear for 1½ minutes each side. Remove from the pan, let cool slightly, then slice thickly.

✧ Arrange the pasta salad on 4 serving plates and top each with a warm salmon slice. Spoon the saffron salsa over and around the salmon and pasta and serve garnished with basil leaves.

linguine
with shrimp

¼ cup (2 fl oz/60 ml) olive oil

3 cloves garlic, crushed

6 golden (French) shallots, peeled
and thinly sliced

1½ lb (750 g) uncooked shrimp
(prawns), peeled and deveined

½ cup (4 fl oz/125 ml) dry vermouth

2 cups (16 fl oz/500 ml) homemade
or purchased tomato pasta sauce

½ cup (3 oz/90 g) drained oil-packed
sun-dried tomatoes, shredded

2 tablespoons fresh basil leaves or
oregano, shredded, plus extra whole
leaves, to garnish

1 lb (500 g) dried linguine

salt and ground black pepper

◈ Warm the oil in a large pan over medium heat. Add the garlic and shallot and cook, stirring, until soft, 3–4 minutes. Increase the heat to high, add the shrimp, and cook, tossing, until they turn pink and curl up, 2–3 minutes.

◈ Stir in the vermouth, pasta sauce, sun-dried tomatoes, and basil. Reduce the heat and simmer until the sauce thickens slightly, about 5 minutes.

◈ Meanwhile, cook the pasta in boiling salted water until tender. Drain and return to the pan. Add the sauce and toss gently over low heat until well combined.

◈ Add salt and pepper to taste and divide among serving plates. Top with oregano or basil leaves.

pasta with seafood

serves 4–6

1 lb (500 g) dried linguine

7 oz (200 g) smoked salmon

1 large red bell pepper
(capsicum), roasted

2 ripe tomatoes

¼ cup (2 fl oz/60 ml) olive oil

2 cloves garlic, crushed

1 fresh red chile, minced

1 lb (500 g) uncooked shrimp
(prawns), peeled and deveined

½ cup (4 fl oz/125 ml) white
wine (optional)

1 avocado, peeled and diced

½ cup (½ oz/15 g) fresh small
basil leaves

salt and ground black pepper

½ cup (2 oz/60 g) walnuts,
toasted and chopped

◈ Cook the pasta in boiling salted water until tender.

◈ Meanwhile, slice the salmon into slivers. Peel the bell pepper and slice into thin strips. Peel, seed, and dice the tomatoes.

◈ Warm the oil in a large frying pan over medium-high heat. Add the garlic and chile and cook, stirring, until the garlic is light golden, 2–3 minutes. Add the shrimp and cook, tossing, until they turn pink and curl up, about 3 minutes. Add the smoked salmon, bell pepper, tomato, and wine, if using. Reduce the heat to low and cook, tossing gently, until heated through.

◈ Drain the pasta and return it to the pan. Add the sauce, avocado, basil, and salt and pepper to taste. Toss gently over low heat until well combined. Spoon into serving bowls, top with walnuts, and serve immediately.

lobster fettuccine

1/4 cup (2 oz oz/60 g) butter

1 onion, finely chopped

2 cloves garlic, crushed

1 lb (500 g) uncooked lobster meat, chopped

salt and ground black pepper

1/4 cup (2 fl oz/60 ml) brandy

1/4 cup (1/4 oz/7 g) chopped fresh parsley

1/4 cup (1/4 oz/7 g) fresh basil leaves, shredded

1/3 cup (3 fl oz/90 ml) homemade or purchased tomato pasta sauce

1/4 cup (2 fl oz/60 ml) light (single) cream

1 lb (500 g) dried fettuccine

Melt the butter in a large frying pan over medium heat. Add the onion and garlic and cook, stirring frequently, until soft, 4–5 minutes. Season the lobster with salt and pepper to taste, add to the pan, and cook until just tender, 3–4 minutes. Increase the heat to high, add the brandy, and flambé if desired.

Stir in the parsley, basil, tomato pasta sauce, and cream. Reduce the heat to medium and cook, stirring occasionally, until heated through, about 5 minutes.

Meanwhile, cook the pasta in boiling salted water until tender. Drain, return to the pan, and add the lobster sauce. Toss gently over low heat until well combined. Season to taste and serve immediately.

penne with bacon and mushrooms

serves 4–6

2 tablespoons olive oil

7 oz (200 g) bacon, chopped

7 oz (200 g) button mushrooms, thinly sliced

2 cloves garlic, crushed

1 small red chile, chopped

1 lb (500 g) ripe tomatoes, peeled and chopped

1 cup (1 oz/30 g) basil leaves, roughly chopped

salt and ground black pepper

1 lb (500 g) dried penne

extra-virgin olive oil

½ cup (2 oz/60 g) grated Parmesan cheese

⬧ Warm the oil in a large frying pan over medium heat. Add the bacon and mushrooms and cook, stirring occasionally, until the bacon begins to brown, about 5 minutes.

⬧ Add the garlic, chile, tomato, and basil, reduce the heat, and simmer until the sauce thickens slightly, 10–15 minutes. Add salt and pepper to taste.

⬧ Meanwhile, cook the pasta in boiling salted water until tender. Drain and return to the saucepan. Stir in extra-virgin olive oil to taste and add the Parmesan cheese.

⬧ Divide the pasta among serving bowls, spoon the sauce over, and serve immediately.

quick and easy
meat
and poultry

char-grilled
chicken breasts

serves 4

4 skinless, boneless
chicken breast halves, each
about 5 oz (155 g)

MARINADE

juice of 1 lemon

2 tablespoons vegetable oil

1/2 teaspoon ground
white pepper

2 teaspoons dried tarragon

fresh tarragon sprigs, to garnish

lemon slices, to garnish

◈ Place the chicken breasts in a glass or ceramic dish.

◈ Combine the lemon juice, oil, pepper, and tarragon in a screwtop jar and shake vigorously to emulsify. Pour over the chicken, cover, and set aside to marinate at room temperature for 20 minutes or in the refrigerator for several hours or overnight.

◈ Preheat a grill (barbecue) or broiler (griller). Cook the chicken over moderate heat until just cooked through, turning once. Test by pressing the thickest part: it should feel firm. Transfer to warmed plates, garnish with tarragon sprigs and lemon slices, and serve immediately.

grilled lemongrass beef

serves 6

1 lb (500 g) beef chuck, rump, or sirloin, in one piece

LEMONGRASS MARINADE

1 tablespoon toasted sesame seeds

2 lemongrass stalks, tender heart section only, finely chopped

3 Asian (purple) shallots, minced

3 cloves garlic

1 small red chile, seeded

1 tablespoon sugar

1½ tablespoons fish sauce

¼ teaspoon ground black pepper

1½ teaspoons toasted (Asian) sesame oil

1 tablespoon peanut or vegetable oil

Lime Dipping Sauce (page 115)

Wrap the beef in plastic wrap and place in the freezer until partially frozen, about 1 hour.

In a blender or mini food processor, combine the sesame seeds, lemongrass, shallots, garlic, chile, and sugar. Process to a smooth paste. Transfer to a large bowl and add the fish sauce, pepper, sesame oil, and peanut or vegetable oil.

Slice the beef very thinly across the grain. Add to the marinade, toss to coat, and leave for at least 1 hour at room temperature, or cover and refrigerate for up to 4 hours.

Preheat a ridged grill pan over medium–high heat until hot and spread the beef slices over it. (Or, prepare a fire in a charcoal grill (barbecue). When the coals are ash white, lay the beef slices flat on the grill rack about 4 inches (10 cm) above the coals.) Cook, turning once, until cooked through, about 30 seconds on each side.

Transfer the beef slices to warmed serving plates and serve with the dipping sauce.

lime dipping sauce

1 clove garlic, crushed

1 small fresh red chile, seeded and minced

1/4 cup (2 oz/60 g) sugar

1/4 cup (2 fl oz/60 ml) fresh lime juice, including pulp

1/4 cup (2 fl oz/60 ml) Thai or Vietnamese fish sauce

1/2 cup (4 fl oz/125 ml) water

In a mortar, combine the garlic, chile, and sugar. Mash with a pestle to form a paste. Add the lime juice and pulp, fish sauce, and water and stir until the sugar is dissolved. Strain the sauce into a bowl and use immediately, or cover tightly and refrigerate for up to 5 days.

**makes 1 1/4 cups
(10 fl oz/310 ml)**

grilled five-spice chicken

serves 4

A popular Chinese spice blend, five-spice powder is a combination of star anise, fennel, cassia, Sichuan peppercorns, and cloves. In this easy Vietnamese recipe, the aromatic powder flavors grilled (barbecued) chicken. Accompany with steamed white rice.

FIVE-SPICE MARINADE

2 teaspoons fresh ginger, peeled and grated

4 cloves garlic, chopped

2 purple (Asian) shallots, chopped

1½ tablespoons brown sugar

½ teaspoon salt

¼ teaspoon ground black pepper

½ teaspoon five-spice powder

2 tablespoons Vietnamese or Thai fish sauce

2 tablespoons soy sauce

1 tablespoon dry sherry

Lime Dipping Sauce (page 115)

4 large skinless, boneless chicken breasts

✧ For the marinade, combine the ginger, garlic, shallot, brown sugar, and salt in a mortar or mini food processor. Mash with a pestle or process to a smooth paste. Transfer to a large, shallow bowl. Add the pepper, five-spice powder, fish sauce, soy sauce, and sherry and stir well. Add the chicken breasts and turn to coat thoroughly with the marinade. Cover and marinate in the refrigerator for a few hours or as long as overnight.

✧ Preheat a grill (barbecue) or broiler (griller) and cook the chicken over moderate heat until just cooked through, turning once. Test by pressing the thickest part: It should feel firm.

✧ Serve hot with the dipping sauce.

pork with crunchy red cabbage

serves 4

8 oz (250 g) red cabbage

6 oz (180 g) red (Spanish) onion

2 red apples

4 thin, lean pork chops, about
1½ lb (700 g) total weight

¼ cup (2 fl oz/60 ml) balsamic vinegar

3 tablespoons chopped fresh herbs,
such as parsley and/or sage

1 tablespoon honey

2 tablespoons lemon juice

salt and ground black pepper

1 tablespoon vegetable oil

1 clove garlic

❖ Finely shred the cabbage; slice the onion and apples. Trim the pork and make criss-cross cuts on one side. In a small bowl, combine half of the balsamic vinegar, all of the chopped herbs, half of the honey, half of the lemon juice, and salt and pepper to taste.

❖ Warm the oil in a large frying pan over medium heat. Add the onions and garlic and sauté for 2 minutes. Add the cabbage, apples, the remaining vinegar, honey, and lemon juice, and salt and pepper to taste. Cook until the liquid has evaporated, 4–5 minutes; keep warm.

❖ Meanwhile, broil (grill) the pork chops for 4–5 minutes on each side, basting with the honey mixture. Serve with the warm cabbage.

chicken
with tarragon cream

serves 6

6 boneless, skinless chicken breast fillets, each about 5 oz (155 g)

salt and ground black pepper

3 tablespoons unsalted butter

1 tablespoon dried tarragon

¾ cup (6 fl oz/185 ml) light (single) cream

❖ Season the chicken breasts with salt and pepper to taste. In a large frying pan over medium heat, melt the butter. Add the chicken and sauté until cooked through and golden brown, about 6 minutes.

❖ Transfer to warmed serving plates and keep warm in a low oven while you make the sauce.

❖ For the sauce, stir the tarragon into the cream. Pour the cream mixture into the pan, reduce the heat, and cook gently for 2–3 minutes. Spoon over the chicken and serve at once.

pork balls
with madeira

serves 4–6

12 oz (375 g) ground (minced) pork

2½ oz (75 g) prosciutto

1 large clove garlic, crushed

1 large slice white bread

salt and ground black pepper

1 medium egg

2 tablespoons vegetable oil

¼ cup (2 fl oz/60 ml) Madeira

½ cup (4 fl oz/125 ml) stock

6 fresh sage leaves, shredded

5 fl oz (150ml) heavy (double) cream

1 lb (500 g) dried linguine

❖ Put the ground pork and prosciutto in a food processor fitted with the metal blade and pulse briefly to chop the prosciutto. Add the garlic, bread, ½ teaspoon salt, pepper to taste, and the egg. Process until well mixed.

❖ Divide the mixture into fourths, then shape 6 meatballs from each portion.

❖ Heat the oil in a large frying pan and fry the meatballs, turning, until golden all over. Add the Madeira and allow to bubble until reduced by half.

❖ Add the stock, sage, and salt and pepper to taste. Reduce the heat and simmer for 5 minutes, then stir in the cream. Warm through; do not allow to boil.

❖ Meanwhile, cook the pasta in boiling salted water until al dente. Drain and return to the pan. Add the meatballs and sauce and toss gently to combine. Serve at once.

pepper steak

serves 2

vegetable oil

two 6-oz (175-g) sirloin or fillet steaks, about ½ inch (1 cm) thick, trimmed and scored

2 teaspoons mixed peppercorns (green, red, and black), crushed

2 small golden (French) shallots, minced

¼ cup (2 fl oz/60 ml) Madeira

⅓ cup (3 fl oz/90 ml) water

2 tablespoons butter, cut into pieces

salt and ground black pepper

◈ Brush a little oil over a small, heavy-based frying pan. Warm the pan over high heat and, when very hot, fry the steaks, allowing 1 minute per side for rare steaks, 2 minutes for medium–rare, 3 minutes for medium, and 4 minutes for well done. Transfer to warmed serving plates and place in a low oven.

◈ Cool the pan slightly, then add the pepper, shallot, Madeira, water, and butter. Bring to the boil, stirring occasionally; allow to bubble until the liquid is slightly reduced. Add salt and pepper to taste.

◈ Spoon some of the sauce over the steaks; pass the remainder separately in a small jug.

flavored butters

When you don't have time to marinate your meat or poultry or make a sauce for it, flavored butters are a simple, delicious alternative. They can be made ahead of time and kept, covered, in the refrigerator for up to 4 weeks. Or they can be formed into logs, wrapped in plastic wrap, and frozen for up to 3 months. When needed, simply slice off a little butter, place atop hot cooked meat, fish, or vegetables, and allow to melt, forming an instant sauce.

mustard and horseradish butter

This butter is best with red meats.

1 cup (8 oz/250 g) butter, softened

1 clove garlic, crushed

2 tablespoons seeded mustard

1 tablespoon horseradish cream

2 tablespoons chopped fresh chives

1 tablespoon chopped fresh rosemary

◈ Place the butter, garlic, mustard, and horseradish cream in the bowl of a food processor fitted with the metal blade and process until combined.

◈ Transfer to a bowl and stir in the chives and rosemary. Spoon into a serving dish, cover, and refrigerate until firm. For longer storage, chilled butter may be formed into a log, wrapped in plastic wrap, and frozen.

makes 1¼ cups (10 oz/315 g)

herb and lime butter

This butter is suitable to serve with meat, fish, and poultry, or to baste steaks while they are on the grill (barbecue). Or try it with steamed vegetables.

1 cup (8 oz/250 g) butter, softened

1 tablespoon grated lime zest

2 tablespoons lime juice

1 clove garlic, crushed

2 shallots, chopped

2 tablespoons chopped parsley

2 tablespoons chopped chives

1 tablespoon chopped tarragon

❖ Place all the ingredients in the bowl of a food processor fitted with the metal blade and process until combined.

❖ Spoon into a serving dish, cover, and refrigerate until firm. For longer storage, chilled butter may be formed into a log, wrapped in plastic wrap, and frozen.

makes 1¼ cups (10 oz/315 g)

chile ginger butter

This butter is suitable for meat, fish, poultry, or vegetables.

1 cup (8 oz/250 g) butter, softened

1 clove garlic, crushed

2 teaspoons chile oil

1 teaspoon chopped red or green chile

1 tablespoon grated fresh ginger

2 teaspoons paprika

1 tablespoon tomato paste

❖ Place all the ingredients in the bowl of a food processor fitted with the metal blade and process until combined.

❖ Spoon into a serving dish, cover, and refrigerate until firm. For longer storage, chilled butter may be formed into a log, wrapped in plastic wrap, and frozen.

makes 1¼ cups (10 oz/315 g)

yogurt-marinated chicken kabobs

serves 4

The yogurt in this classic marinade tenderizes the chicken, yielding succulent results. If you like, cook vegetables on separate skewers so their cooking can be easily monitored. Serve the kabobs with pita bread or pilaf and spoon some yogurt sauce (page 157) or purchased tzatziki over the vegetable skewers.

1 large yellow onion, chopped

4 cloves garlic, minced

¼ cup (2 fl oz/60 ml) fresh lemon juice

1 tablespoon paprika

½ teaspoon cayenne pepper

½ teaspoon ground black pepper, plus extra to taste

1 tablespoon chopped fresh thyme

1 cup (8 oz/250 g) plain yogurt

1½ lb (750 g) boneless, skinless chicken meat

olive oil, for brushing

salt

❖ In a food processor fitted with the metal blade or in a blender, combine the onion, garlic, lemon juice, paprika, cayenne, ½ teaspoon black pepper, and thyme. Using rapid on-off pulses, process until well combined. Add the yogurt and pulse to mix.

❖ Rinse the chicken and pat dry. Cut into 1-inch (2.5-cm) cubes and place in a glass or ceramic dish. Pour the yogurt mixture over the chicken and turn to coat. Cover and marinate in the refrigerator for 8 hours or overnight.

❖ Prepare a fire in a charcoal grill (barbecue) or preheat a broiler (griller).

❖ Remove the chicken pieces from the marinade, reserving the marinade, and thread them onto four oiled metal skewers. Brush chicken with olive oil, then sprinkle with salt and pepper.

❖ Place the skewers on an oiled grill rack or a broiler pan and grill or broil, turning and basting once with the reserved marinade, until no longer pink in the center when cut into with a knife, 4–5 minutes per side for breast meat and 5–6 minutes per side for thigh meat.

❖ Transfer the skewers to warmed individual plates or a platter. Serve hot.

beef rolls
with blue cheese sauce

serves 4

Even those who normally
dislike blue cheese may be
won over by the rich, winey
sauce that accompanies this
dish. For a subtly flavored
sauce, try a blue Brie.
A sharp blue cheese, such
as Stilton or Roquefort,
will give a stronger flavor.

8 thin beef or veal steaks (about 1¼ lb/625 g in total)

8 spears fresh asparagus

8 thin slices cooked ham or prosciutto

1 tablespoon olive oil

BLUE CHEESE SAUCE

2 tablespoons butter

1½ tablespoons all-purpose (plain) flour

¼ cup (2 fl oz/60 ml) dry white wine

1 cup (8 fl oz/250 ml) milk

¾ cup (3 oz/90 g) blue cheese (see note)

¼ cup (1 oz/30 g) grated Cheddar cheese

salt and ground white pepper

✥ Preheat a broiler (griller).

✥ Place the steaks between two sheets of plastic wrap and pound lightly with the flat side of a meat mallet until evenly thick.

✥ Trim the asparagus spears to even lengths and parboil in lightly salted water for 3 minutes. Drain, refresh under cold running water, and drain again.

✥ Place a slice of ham or prosciutto and an asparagus spear on each steak. Roll up the steak, secure with toothpicks, and brush with oil. Broil (grill), turning frequently, until the meat is done to your liking.

✥ Meanwhile, make the cheese sauce. Melt the butter in a small pan over medium heat, add the flour, and cook, stirring, for 1–2 minutes. Stir in the wine and milk, increase the temperature, and boil, stirring continuously, until thickened. Add the cheeses and salt and pepper to taste and cook over medium heat until the cheeses melt and the sauce is creamy.

✥ Arrange the rolls on warmed serving plates and pour on the sauce, or serve separately.

japanese
chicken kabobs

serves 4

Serve these as appetizers, too—warm or chilled. Allow 1 kabob per serving. As a main course, offer the kabobs on a bed of fluffy steamed white rice. When weather permits, cook the kabobs on the grill (barbecue) instead of under the broiler (griller).

1 teaspoon finely grated orange zest

1/2 cup (4 fl oz/125 ml) orange juice

1/3 cup (3 fl oz/90 ml) dry sherry

1/4 cup (2 fl oz/60 ml) soy sauce

2 teaspoons sugar

1 clove garlic, minced

1/2 teaspoon peeled and grated fresh ginger

12 oz (375 g) boneless, skinless chicken breast halves

6–8 green (spring) onions

hot cooked rice, to serve

pickled ginger (optional)

❖ In a small mixing bowl, combine the orange zest, orange juice, sherry, soy sauce, sugar, garlic, and ginger. Set aside ¼ cup (2 fl oz/60 ml) of the marinade mixture to serve with the cooked kabobs.

❖ Cut the chicken breast halves into 1-inch (2.5-cm) cubes. Cut the green onions into 1½-inch (4-cm) lengths. Lightly oil 4 metal skewers. Thread chicken pieces and onion pieces onto the skewers, alternating chicken and onions. Place the kabobs in a shallow dish and pour the marinade over the kabobs. Marinate at room temperature for 30 minutes, turning kabobs once. Remove kabobs from marinade, reserving marinade.

❖ Preheat a broiler (griller). Place the kabobs on the unheated rack of a broiler pan. Broil, 4 inches (10 cm) from the heat, until chicken is tender and no pink remains, 8–10 minutes. Turn and brush with marinade once. Discard remaining marinade.

❖ Meanwhile, heat the ¼ cup (2 fl oz/60 ml) reserved marinade. Serve the kabobs with rice, warmed marinade, and pickled ginger, if desired.

dry-fried
sweet spiced beef

serves 4

1½ lb (700 g) rump steak

1½-inch (4-cm) piece fresh ginger, peeled and finely chopped

½ teaspoon hot-pepper sauce, or to taste

½ teaspoon ground cumin

2 tablespoons dark brown sugar

3 tablespoons vegetable oil

6 oz (180 g) thinly sliced onion

3 tablespoons lemon juice

⅓ cup (3 fl oz/90 ml) beef stock or water

salt and ground black pepper

chopped fresh chives, to garnish (optional)

hot Singapore-style noodles, to serve

◈ Cut the beef into wafer-thin, bite-size slices. In a bowl, combine the beef, ginger, hot-pepper sauce, cumin, and sugar.

◈ Warm the oil in a wok over medium–high heat. Add the onion and stir-fry until golden brown, 3–4 minutes. Add the beef mixture and stir-fry until just browned and tender, 4–5 minutes longer.

◈ Add the lemon juice and stock. Bring to a boil and allow to bubble until slightly reduced. Add salt and pepper to taste.

◈ Garnish with chives, if desired, and serve immediately atop hot noodles.

wine-based marinades

red wine and mustard

Suitable for red meat and game.

1¼ cups (10 fl oz/300 ml) red wine
1 cup (8 fl oz/250 ml) olive oil
¼ cup (2 fl oz/60 ml) port
2 tablespoons balsamic vinegar
2 tablespoons Dijon mustard
1 onion, sliced
1 clove garlic, crushed
1 bay leaf, crumbled
2–3 sprigs parsley
1 tablespoon brown sugar
several black peppercorns

❖ Combine all ingredients in a shallow glass or ceramic dish. Add meat and turn to coat well. Marinate, covered, in the refrigerator for several hours or overnight. Brush meat with marinade during cooking.

makes 3 cups (24 fl oz/750 ml)

wine and herb

Suitable for poultry, seafood, and fish.

1½ cups (12 fl oz/375 ml) olive oil
1 cup (8 fl oz/250 ml) dry white wine
½ cup (4 fl oz/125 ml) dry vermouth
½ cup (4 fl oz/125 ml) lemon juice
2 cloves garlic, crushed
6 golden (French) shallots, chopped
2 tablespoons lemon thyme, crumbled
2–3 sprigs parsley
2 tablespoons chopped dill
1 lemon, sliced

❖ Combine all ingredients in a shallow glass or ceramic dish. Add poultry, seafood, or fish and turn to coat well. Marinate, covered, in the refrigerator for several hours. Brush poultry, seafood, or fish with marinade during cooking.

makes 4 cups (1 qt/1 liter)

sautéed chicken with
beurre blanc

serves 4

Beurre blanc, a famous
French sauce, breaks down
easily and cannot be
reheated. If it turns oily,
beat a spoonful of it in a
chilled bowl until creamy,
then add the rest of the
sauce a spoonful at a time.

4 boneless, skinless chicken breast halves
(about 1 lb/500 g total)

1 tablespoon olive oil or vegetable oil

salt and pepper

2 tablespoons finely chopped golden (French) shallot
or green (spring) onion

1/4 cup (2 fl oz/60 ml) sherry wine vinegar or white
wine vinegar

1/4 cup (2 fl oz/60 ml) dry sherry

1 tablespoon whipping cream

1/3 cup (3 oz/90 g) butter (at room temperature),
cut into 6 pieces

1/8 teaspoon ground white pepper

✧ Rinse the chicken and pat dry. Warm the oil in a large frying pan over medium–high heat. Add the chicken and cook, turning once, until tender and no pink remains, 10–12 minutes. Sprinkle chicken with salt and pepper to taste, place on serving plates, and keep warm in a low oven while preparing the sauce.

✧ Meanwhile, in a small, heavy saucepan over medium heat, combine the shallot or green onion, vinegar, and dry sherry. Bring to a boil and cook, uncovered, until the liquid is reduced to about 1 tablespoon.

✧ With a wire whisk, whisk in the whipping cream, reduce the heat, and boil gently until thickened, 2–3 minutes. Remove the pan from the heat.

✧ Whisk in the butter, 1 piece at a time, allowing each piece to melt completely before adding the next. Stir in the pepper. If desired, strain the sauce to remove the shallots.

✧ Spoon the sauce over the chicken and serve immediately.

sherried chicken

serves 4

4 boneless, skinless chicken breast
halves (about 1 lb/500 g total)

¼ cup (1¼ oz/35 g) all-purpose
(plain) flour

½ teaspoon salt

¼ teaspoon ground white pepper

2 tablespoons vegetable oil

1 clove garlic, cut into thin slivers

½ cup (4 fl oz/125 ml) cream sherry

1 cup (8 fl oz/250 ml) orange juice

2 tablespoons orange marmalade

¼ cup (1 oz/30 g) sliced
almonds, toasted

hot cooked white rice, to serve

❖ Rinse chicken and pat dry. In a large plastic bag, combine the flour, salt, and pepper. Add the chicken, 1 piece at a time, shaking bag to coat chicken with flour mixture. In a large frying pan over medium heat, warm the oil. Add the chicken and cook, turning once, until tender and no pink remains, 10–12 minutes. Transfer chicken to serving plates and keep warm in a low oven.

❖ Add the garlic to the pan drippings and cook, stirring, for 15 seconds. Carefully add the cream sherry, bring to a boil, and cook gently, uncovered, until the liquid is reduced by half, 1–2 minutes. Stir in the orange juice and marmalade. Bring to a boil and cook gently, uncovered, until slightly thickened, 2–3 minutes. Pour over the chicken and sprinkle with toasted almonds. Serve with hot rice.

chicken
with sage and thyme

serves 2–4

2 chicken thigh fillets, skinned
and trimmed of fat

2 boneless, skinless
chicken breast halves

¼ cup (2 oz/60 g)
unsalted butter, melted

1 teaspoon dried sage

1 teaspoon dried thyme

salt and ground black pepper

❖ Slit the underside of each thigh, if necessary, so that the meat lies flat. Place between two sheets of waxed paper and, using the flat side of a meat mallet, pound until the meat is of an even thickness, about ⅛ inch (3 mm). Do the same with the chicken breast fillets.

❖ Brush both sides of each chicken piece with the melted butter, then sprinkle with the sage and thyme.

❖ Warm a heavy frying pan over high heat until very hot. Add the chicken and cook quickly, 1–2 minutes on each side. Season to taste with salt and pepper, transfer to warmed plates, and serve at once.

chicken diana

serves 4

4 boneless, skinless
chicken breast halves
(about 1 lb/500 g total)

2 tablespoons butter

2 golden (French)
shallots, finely chopped

2 tablespoons brandy

½ cup (4 fl oz/125 ml)
chicken stock

2 tablespoons
white wine

dash of Worcestershire
sauce

1 teaspoon Dijon
mustard

2 tablespoons chopped
fresh parsley

❖ Rinse the chicken and pat dry. Place each breast half between two pieces of plastic wrap. Working from the center to the edges, pound chicken lightly with the flat side of a meat mallet to a ¼-inch (5-mm) even thickness. Remove the plastic wrap.

❖ In a large frying pan, melt the butter. Add the shallot and cook over medium heat until tender. Increase the heat to medium–high, add the chicken, and cook until tender and no pink remains, 4–6 minutes, turning once. Remove pan from heat. Sprinkle the chicken with the brandy. Ignite the brandy using a very long match while keeping your hand to the side of the skillet. When the flame is gone, transfer the chicken to warmed serving plates and keep warm in a low oven.

❖ Add the stock, wine, Worcestershire sauce, and mustard to the pan. Bring to a boil, then boil gently until liquid is slightly thickened and reduced by half, about 5 minutes. Pour sauce over chicken breasts, sprinkle with parsley, and serve at once.

spiced coconut lamb

serves 4

1 small onion, roughly chopped

1 red chile, stemmed and seeded

2 tablespoons vegetable oil

2 cloves garlic

1 oz (25 g) blanched almonds

½ teaspoon ground turmeric

½ teaspoon ground ginger

*8 lean lamb cutlets,
about 1 lb (500 g) total weight*

juice of 1 lemon

1 stalk lemongrass

1 teaspoon dark brown sugar

1 cup (8 fl oz/250 ml) coconut milk

⅔ cup (5 fl oz/150 ml) water

salt and ground black pepper

chopped cilantro (fresh coriander) leaves

❖ In a food processor, process the onion, chile, oil, garlic, almonds, and spices to a paste. Fry the paste in a large frying pan or wok, stirring constantly, for 1–2 minutes. Add the cutlets and cook over medium heat until well browned on both sides.

❖ Stir in the lemon juice, lemongrass, sugar, coconut milk, and water. Bring to a boil, cover, reduce heat, and simmer gently until cutlets are tender, about 15 minutes. Uncover and let the liquid bubble until it reduces slightly and thickens to a coating consistency, 3–4 minutes. Stir occasionally to prevent the sauce from sticking to the pan.

❖ Remove the lemongrass and add salt and pepper to taste. Serve at once, garnished with chopped cilantro.

mixed
meat kabobs

12 oz (375 g) lean tender beef (tenderloin, fillet, or rump)

2 tablespoons light soy sauce

2 teaspoons sugar

1 tablespoon dry sherry or brandy

salt and ground black pepper

6 baby lamb cutlets, bone trimmed

1 clove garlic, crushed

3 sheeps' kidneys

3 slices (rashers) fat bacon

3 spicy sausages (such as Italian sausages)

1 large boneless, skinless chicken breast half

2 tablespoons olive or vegetable oil

lemon pepper

6 small bay leaves

6 button mushrooms

6 large cherry tomatoes

2 tablespoons olive oil or melted butter

❖ Cut the beef into 1-inch (2.5-cm) cubes. In a shallow bowl, combine the soy sauce, sugar, sherry or brandy, and salt and pepper to taste. Add the beef cubes, turn to coat the meat with the mixture, and leave to marinate at room temperature for 20 minutes.

❖ Meanwhile, rub the lamb cutlets with garlic and set aside. Cut the kidneys in halves, remove the core, and wrap a half slice of bacon around each. Cut the sausages in halves and set aside. Cut the chicken crosswise into six pieces and rub with oil, then sprinkle with lemon pepper.

❖ When the beef has been marinated, thread all the meats alternately on oiled metal skewers, adding a bay leaf, mushroom, and tomato to each. Brush with oil or melted butter and grill (barbecue) or broil (grill), turning frequently, until done to your liking. Serve immediately.

spiced meatballs

serves 4

1¼ lb (625 g) finely ground (minced) beef or lamb

1 medium onion, grated and drained

2 cloves garlic, crushed

1½ teaspoons dried mint

1 teaspoon salt

½ teaspoon ground black pepper

1½ teaspoons ground cumin

⅓ teaspoon allspice

1 small egg, well beaten

vegetable oil or melted ghee

ACCOMPANIMENTS

thinly sliced onion

2 very ripe tomatoes

plain yogurt or Yogurt Sauce (page 157)

sprigs of mint (optional)

⟡ In a bowl, combine the meat, onion, garlic, mint, salt, pepper, cumin, and allspice. Add the egg and blend thoroughly with your hands, kneading to a smooth consistency. Form into croquette shapes about 2 inches (5 cm) long.

⟡ Preheat a grill (barbecue) or broiler (griller). Oil 4 metal skewers. Thread a skewer lengthwise through the meatballs, placing 3 on each for main course servings, 2 for appetizers. Brush with oil or melted ghee and broil (grill) or grill (barbecue), turning frequently, until cooked through and crisp on the surface.

⟡ Separate the onion into rings (if you like, marinate them for a few minutes in a mixture of vinegar, sugar, and salt). Cut the tomatoes in halves and squeeze out the seeds; very finely dice the flesh and season lightly with salt and pepper. Serve the meatballs on a warmed platter with the accompaniments. Garnish with the mint sprigs, if desired.

recipe tip

Wooden skewers may be used in this recipe, but be sure to soak them in water for at least 1 hour before using them. This will prevent them from burning.

The meatballs can be made in advance on wooden skewers, wrapped tightly in plastic wrap, and frozen. Thaw for 30 minutes before cooking.

sesame chicken with vegetables

serves 6

SAUCE

½ cup (4 fl oz/125 ml) chicken stock

2 tablespoons soy sauce

1 tablespoon toasted (Asian) sesame oil

4 cloves garlic, minced

2 teaspoons peeled and grated fresh ginger

2 teaspoons cornstarch (cornflour)

1 teaspoon sugar

CHICKEN

½ cup (2½ oz/75 g) all-purpose (plain) flour

2 tablespoons sesame seeds

½ teaspoon salt

¼ teaspoon ground red pepper

1 egg, beaten

¼ cup (2 fl oz/60 ml) milk

vegetable oil, for deep-frying

1 lb (500 g) boneless, skinless chicken thighs, cut into ¾-inch (2-cm) pieces

VEGETABLES

1 tablespoon vegetable oil

2 zucchini (courgettes), cut into thin, bite-sized strips

1 green bell pepper (capsicum), cut into thin, bite-sized strips

6 green (spring) onions, bias-sliced into ½-inch (1-cm) pieces

For the sauce, combine the chicken stock, soy sauce, sesame oil, garlic, ginger, cornstarch, and sugar in a small bowl. Set aside.

For the chicken, combine the flour, sesame seeds, salt, and ground red pepper in a large mixing bowl. In a small mixing bowl, combine the egg and milk. Add the liquid mixture to the dry ingredients and beat until smooth.

In a wok or large saucepan, pour in 1½ inches (4 cm) of oil and heat to 365°F (185°C) on a deep-frying thermometer. Dip the chicken, one piece at a time, into the coating, then add to the hot oil. Fry a few pieces of chicken at a time until golden, about 4 minutes. Using a slotted spoon, remove chicken from oil and drain on paper towels. Keep warm in a low oven while stir-frying the vegetables.

For the vegetables, pour a thin layer of vegetable oil into a large frying pan. (Add more oil as necessary during cooking.) Warm the oil over medium–high heat. When hot, add the zucchini, bell pepper, and green onion and stir-fry until crisp-tender, about 3 minutes. Push the vegetables to the side of the pan. Stir the sauce and add to the pan. Cook, stirring, until thickened and bubbly. Cook for 1 minute more.

Return the cooked chicken to the pan containing the vegetables and stir well to combine all the ingredients. Serve immediately.

mustard steaks

serves 2

two 6-oz (175-g) sirloin
or fillet steaks, about
1/2 inch (1 cm) thick

vegetable oil

2 small golden (French) shallots,
finely chopped

2 cloves garlic, crushed

salt and ground black pepper

1/3 cup (3 fl oz/90 ml) light
(single) cream

1/4 cup (2 fl oz/60 ml) brandy

1 tablespoon Dijon mustard

3 oz (90 g) mixed mushrooms

1/4 cup (2 fl oz/60 ml) water

slices of French bread, to serve
(optional)

❖ Trim the steaks and lightly score the flesh.

❖ Brush a little oil over a small, heavy-based frying pan. Heat the pan and, when it is very hot, fry the steaks, allowing 1 minute each side for medium rare, 3 minutes each side for medium, and 4 minutes for well done. Place the steaks on heated plates and keep them warm in a low oven while you make the sauce.

❖ Cool the frying pan slightly, then add the shallots, garlic, salt and pepper to taste, cream, brandy, mustard, mushrooms, and water. Bring just to a boil, stirring occasionally. Reduce the heat and allow the liquid to bubble until slightly reduced and thickened.

❖ Serve the steaks on slices of French bread, if desired. Spoon a little of the sauce over the steaks. Pass the remaining sauce separately.

glazed ham
and mango

oil or melted butter

4 thick ham steaks

1½ tablespoons brown sugar

2 tablespoons butter

salt and ground black pepper

2 fresh medium mangoes

❖ Cut four pieces of aluminum foil, each 12 inches (30 cm) square. Brush with oil or melted butter. Place a steak on each. Make a paste with the brown sugar, butter, and salt and pepper to taste. Spread the paste thickly over the top of each steak. Peel and thickly slice the mangoes and spread slices evenly over each steak, using half a mango for each. Wrap the foil around the parcels and fold edges together to seal.

❖ Place under the broiler (griller) or on a grill (barbecue) rack and cook for about 6 minutes. Alternatively, place on a baking sheet and cook in a 450°F (220°C/Gas Mark 6) oven for 15 minutes.

pork
with bamboo shoots

serves 4

Bamboo shoots are a common ingredient in Chinese dishes, adding a delicate crunch. The fresh shoots may be found in Asian markets; if they are unavailable, substitute drained canned bamboo shoots, which are stocked by most supermarkets.

MARINADE

2 tablespoons light soy sauce

2 teaspoons Chinese rice wine (available at Chinese stores) or dry sherry

1½ teaspoons cornstarch (cornflour)

10 oz (315 g) lean pork, sliced across the grain into fine 1½-inch (4-cm) long strips

¼ cup (2 fl oz/60 ml) peanut oil

5 oz (150 g) bamboo shoots, sliced into fine 1½-inch (4-cm) long strips

1 tablespoon light soy sauce

1 teaspoon sugar

4 green (spring) onions, mainly white parts, cut into 1-inch (2.5-cm) lengths

♦ Combine the soy sauce, rice wine or sherry, and cornstarch in a shallow dish. Add the pork, turn to coat well, and set aside to marinate for 15 minutes.

♦ Pour the peanut oil into a preheated wok or large frying pan and heat until the oil begins to smoke. Stir-fry the pork slices until the color changes, 1–2 minutes. Remove with a slotted spoon and transfer to a plate.

♦ Add the bamboo shoots and toss quickly around the hot pan for 10–15 seconds. Add the soy sauce and sugar, lower the heat, and simmer for 4–5 minutes, stirring occasionally. Raise the heat to high. Return the pork to the pan and toss quickly with the other ingredients until just heated through.

♦ Add the green onion and stir-fry for 1 minute. Serve immediately.

food fact

The delicately flavored bamboo shoot has been eaten in China for about 2000 years. It is considered a particular delicacy in winter, when it has a more pronounced flavor than the spring bamboo shoot. The latter is more delicate in taste and has a crunchier texture.

serves 6

1 lb (500 g) lean tender beef (tenderloin, fillet, or rump), cut into 1-inch (2.5-cm) cubes

1 small onion, grated

1–2 cloves garlic, crushed

1 teaspoon grated ginger

2 tablespoons vegetable oil

1 tablespoon dark soy sauce

¼ teaspoon salt

½ teaspoon ground black pepper

4–6 large green (spring) onions

vegetable oil or melted butter, extra

MINTED COCONUT CHUTNEY

1 cup (1½ oz/45 g) fresh mint leaves

1 onion

½ cup (1 oz/30 g) grated dried (desiccated) coconut

¼ teaspoon black mustard seeds (optional)

¼ cup (2 fl oz/60 ml) white vinegar

2–3 tablespoons sugar

salt to taste

❖ Place the meat in a large dish. Combine the onion, garlic, ginger, oil, soy sauce, salt, and pepper and mix well. Brush the meat with the mixture. Cover the meat with plastic wrap and set aside for 40 minutes.

❖ Preheat a broiler (griller).

❖ Cut green onions into 1¼-inch (3-cm) lengths. Thread the meat pieces onto oiled metal skewers, alternating with the onion pieces. Brush with the extra oil or butter and grill (broil), turning frequently, until done to your liking.

❖ Meanwhile, make the chutney. In a food processor, finely chop the mint leaves; remove. Process the onion to a smooth paste, add the remaining ingredients and the chopped mint, and process until well mixed. Serve the kabobs accompanied with the chutney.

beef kabobs
with minted coconut
chutney

chicken and potato salad with olive mayonnaise

serves 4

OLIVE MAYONNAISE

1 egg yolk

2 tablespoons lemon juice

1 clove garlic

½ teaspoon mustard powder

¼ teaspoon salt

⅛ teaspoon chili powder

1 cup (8 fl oz/250 ml) salad oil

14-oz (440-g) jar pitted green or black olives, drained and finely chopped (use black olives if you prefer a milder flavor)

SALAD

1 lb (500 g) whole tiny new potatoes

salt

2 cups (12 oz/375 g) cooked chicken, cut into ¾-inch (2-cm) cubes

½ cup (2½ oz/75 g) finely chopped red bell pepper (capsicum)

¼ cup (1 oz/30 g) finely chopped green (spring) onion

mixed salad leaves, to serve

❖ For the olive mayonnaise, in a food processor bowl or blender container combine the egg yolk, lemon juice, garlic, mustard, salt, and chili powder. Process until smooth. With the motor running, add the oil in a thin, steady stream. (From time to time, stop the machine and use a rubber spatula to scrape down the sides of the bowl.) Fold through the chopped olives. Set aside 1 cup (8 fl oz/250 ml) of the mayonnaise. Cover and store the remainder in the refrigerator for up to 1 week.

❖ For the salad, cut the unpeeled potatoes into quarters. Place in a medium saucepan; add boiling water to cover and salt to taste. Cover the pan and cook until the potatoes are tender, 10–15 minutes; drain.

❖ In a large mixing bowl, stir together the potatoes, the 1 cup (8 fl oz/250 ml) olive mayonnaise, the cooked chicken, red bell pepper, and green onion. Cover and chill for at least 2 hours. Serve on salad leaves.

151

pork chops
with tangy chutney

serves 4

4 large pork chops

½ teaspoon salt

⅓ teaspoon
black pepper

3 tablespoons
fruit chutney

1 teaspoon vindaloo
paste or other
hot curry sauce

2–3 tablespoons
vegetable oil

hot cooked couscous,
to serve

cucumber salad,
to serve

❖ Preheat a broiler (griller).

❖ Trim excess fat from the pork chops and season them
with salt and pepper. Make a paste with the chutney and
vindaloo or curry paste and brush over both sides of each
chop. Set the remainder aside.

❖ Broil (grill) on medium heat, turning frequently and
brushing with oil. When the chops are almost done,
spread the remaining chutney thickly over one side and
continue to cook on the other side until done.

❖ Serve with couscous and a cucumber salad.

chicken breasts
with sage

serves 4

*4 skinless, boneless
chicken breast halves*

*¼ cup (1½ oz/45 g)
all-purpose (plain) flour*

1 teaspoon dried sage

*3 tablespoons
unsalted butter*

*½ cup (4 fl oz/125 ml)
dry vermouth or
chicken stock*

*1 tablespoon fresh
lemon juice*

salt and ground black pepper

finely grated zest of 1 lemon

❖ Place the chicken breasts between 2 sheets of waxed paper and, using the flat side of a meal mallet, lightly pound to flatten them slightly and evenly.

❖ Combine the flour and sage. Dust the chicken breasts lightly with the flour mixture, then shake off the excess.

❖ Melt the butter in a sauté pan over medium–high heat. Add the chicken breasts and sauté, turning as they become golden, for 2–3 minutes on each side. Transfer to a warmed platter; keep warm.

❖ Pour the vermouth or stock into the pan and bring to a boil over high heat. Deglaze the pan by stirring to dislodge any browned bits; boil until the sauce is reduced by one half, 2–3 minutes. Add the lemon juice and season to taste with salt and pepper.

❖ Pour the sauce over the chicken, sprinkle with the lemon zest, and serve at once.

155

turkish meatballs

serves 6

YOGURT SAUCE

2 cups (1 lb/500 g) thick Greek-style plain yogurt

2 large cloves garlic, finely minced

1½ tablespoons olive oil

1 tablespoon red wine vinegar or fresh lemon juice, or to taste

¼ cup (⅓ oz/10 g) chopped fresh mint

salt and ground black pepper

ONION SALAD

½ lb (250 g) red (Spanish) or white onions

1 tablespoon salt

½ cup (¾ oz/20 g) chopped fresh flat-leaf (Italian) parsley

1 teaspoon sumac (optional; see Glossary, page 313)

MEATBALLS

2 lb (1 kg) ground (minced) lean lamb or beef

2 yellow or red (Spanish) onions, grated (about 1½ cups/7½ oz/235 g)

2 cloves garlic, finely minced

2 eggs

1 tablespoon chopped fresh thyme

1 teaspoon ground black pepper

½ teaspoon salt, plus extra to taste

olive oil, for brushing

6 pita breads, warmed

turkish meatballs

❖ Combine the yogurt, garlic, olive oil, and vinegar or lemon juice. Stir well and fold in the mint. Season to taste with salt and pepper. Cover and refrigerate until needed.

❖ To make the onion salad, cut any large onions in half and then thinly slice all of the onions. Place the onion slices in a large sieve or colander, add the salt, and toss well. Let stand for 15 minutes. Rinse the onion slices with cool water and pat dry with paper towels. Place in a bowl and add the parsley and the sumac, if using. Toss well; set aside.

❖ Preheat a broiler (griller) or a gas or electric grill (barbecue), or prepare a fire in a charcoal grill.

❖ To make the meatballs, combine the lamb or beef, grated onions, garlic, eggs, thyme, pepper, and the ½ teaspoon salt in a bowl. Mix with your hands until the mixture holds together well. Form into 12 ovals, each about 3 inches (7.5 cm) long and 1½ inches (4 cm) wide, and thread them onto oiled metal skewers.

❖ Brush the meatballs with olive oil and sprinkle with salt to taste. Broil (grill) or grill (barbecue), turning to brown on all sides, until cooked through, about 8 minutes.

❖ Slip the meatballs off the skewers. Cut the pita breads in halves and tuck a meatball into each half. Serve at once, accompanied with the yogurt sauce and onion salad.

beer-marinated sausages

serves 4–5

2 cups (16 fl oz/500 ml) beer

½ cup (4 fl oz/125 ml) olive or
vegetable oil

½ cup (4 fl oz/125 ml) ketchup
(tomato sauce)

2 tablespoons Worcestershire
sauce

¼ cup (2 fl oz/60 ml)
Dijon mustard

1 onion, chopped

1 clove garlic, peeled

½ teaspoon cracked
black pepper

10 pork or beef sausages

❖ Combine the beer, oil, ketchup, Worcestershire sauce, mustard, onion, garlic, and pepper in a large shallow dish.

❖ With a fork, prick the sausages well. Add to the dish containing the marinade and turn to coat well. Cover and allow to marinate in the refrigerator for several hours or overnight.

❖ Drain sausages from marinade, reserving marinade. Grill (barbecue) or broil (grill) the sausages, turning frequently and brushing with marinade, until cooked through, 10–15 minutes. Serve immediately. Discard any remaining marinade.

sichuan pork
and peanuts

MARINADE

a little egg white

2 teaspoons cornstarch (cornflour)

1 tablespoon water

*1 lb (500 g) pork tenderloin or fillet,
cut into ¾-inch (2-cm) dice*

SAUCE

*1 tablespoon Chinese rice wine
or dry sherry*

1½ tablespoons light soy sauce

1 teaspoon salt

1 teaspoon sugar

1 teaspoon chile bean paste

1 teaspoon cornstarch (cornflour)

*½ teaspoon brown bean paste (optional;
see note on page 161)*

¼ cup (2 fl oz/60 ml) peanut oil

1 clove garlic, sliced

3 slices fresh ginger

1 onion, cut into ¾-inch (2-cm) dice

*1 red bell pepper (capsicum),
cut into ¾-inch (2-cm) dice*

*½ cup (4 oz/125 g) roasted or deep-fried
unsalted peanuts*

✧ Combine all of the marinade ingredients in a large shallow dish. Add the pork and turn to coat well. Set aside to marinate while you prepare the other ingredients.

✧ For the sauce, combine the rice wine or sherry, soy sauce, salt, sugar, chile bean paste, cornstarch, and brown bean paste, if using. Set aside.

✧ In a wok or large frying pan over high heat, warm 2 tablespoons of the peanut oil until it is just beginning to smoke. Add the garlic and ginger and stir-fry for a few seconds. Add the onion and bell pepper and toss for a few seconds. Transfer to a plate and set aside.

✧ Wipe out the pan, add the remaining peanut oil, and heat until the oil begins to smoke. Add the pork and its marinade and stir-fry until the pork changes color, 2–3 minutes. Stir the sauce ingredients and add to the pan, stirring to coat the pork. Return the onion and bell pepper mixture to the pan and toss together quickly and thoroughly. Stir in the peanuts. Serve at once.

✧ NOTE: Chinese rice wine, chile bean paste, and brown bean paste (*min si jeung*) are available at Chinese food stores.

lamb
in honey sauce

serves 4

In this Chinese dish, lamb slices are stir-fried in a variety of seasonings, producing a tender and flavorsome result.

Hoisin sauce and Chinese rice wine (sometimes called Shaoxing rice wine) are available at Chinese stores.

½ lb (250 g) lean boneless lamb

1 tablespoon hoisin sauce (see note)

½ teaspoon sesame oil

2 tablespoons cornstarch (cornflour)

3 tablespoons peanut oil

SEASONINGS

1 tablespoon light soy sauce

1 teaspoon brown vinegar

1 teaspoon Chinese rice wine or dry sherry (see note)

1 teaspoon ginger juice (use a garlic press)

1 teaspoon honey

2 teaspoons sugar

½ teaspoon cornstarch (cornflour)

◈ Slice the lamb across the grain into thin slices. Place in a dish, add the hoisin sauce and sesame oil, and mix well. Dust with the cornstarch to coat the meat pieces evenly.

◈ Preheat a wok or large frying pan. Add the peanut oil and heat until moderately hot. Add the lamb and stir-fry for 1–2 minutes, stirring with chopsticks to separate the slices. Remove and drain well.

◈ Pour off all but 1 tablespoon of the oil and stir in all the seasoning ingredients. Bring to a boil. Return the lamb to the wok and stir quickly over high heat until the sauce coats the lamb slices. Serve at once.

food fact

Peanut oil (also known as groundnut oil) is particularly popular in Chinese cooking for stir-frying and deep-frying. It retains a hint of the nut's rich flavor but does not overpower the taste of the other ingredients. Peanut oil, like other nut oils, may also be used to flavor dipping sauces and salad dressings. It is commonly used in blended cooking oils, margarines, and commercial mayonnaises and salad dressings. For stir-frying and deep-frying, most types of vegetable oil may be substituted for it.

chicken
provençal

2 cups (8 oz/250 g) cubed peeled eggplant (aubergine)

2 tomatoes, peeled, seeded, and chopped

1 onion, halved and thinly sliced

1 red bell pepper (capsicum), cut into thin strips

1 green bell pepper (capsicum), cut into thin strips

¼ cup (2 fl oz/60 ml) red or dry white wine or chicken stock

2 tablespoons chopped fresh basil or 1½ teaspoons dried basil, crushed

2 cloves garlic, minced

½ teaspoon salt

4 boneless, skinless chicken breast halves (about 1 lb/500 g total)

salt

1 tablespoon olive oil or vegetable oil

½ teaspoon paprika

✧ In a large saucepan, combine the eggplant, tomato, onion, red and green bell pepper, wine or chicken stock, basil, garlic, and ½ teaspoon salt. Bring to a boil over medium–high heat, then reduce heat and simmer, covered, for 10 minutes. Uncover and simmer for 5 minutes more, or until the vegetables are tender and nearly all of the liquid is evaporated.

✧ Meanwhile, rinse chicken; pat dry. Place each breast half between 2 pieces of plastic wrap. Working from the center to the edges, pound chicken lightly with the flat side of a meat mallet to a ½-inch (1-cm) thickness. Remove plastic wrap. Sprinkle chicken lightly with salt.

✧ In a large frying pan, warm the oil and paprika over medium-high heat. Add the chicken and cook until tender and no pink remains, 4–6 minutes, turning once.

✧ To serve, spoon the vegetable mixture onto warmed serving plates and top with the chicken.

sautéed liver with oregano

serves 4

1¼ lb (625 g) lambs' liver,
trimmed and thinly sliced

1 cup (5 oz/150 g) all-purpose
(plain) flour

salt and ground black pepper

¼ cup (2 fl oz/60 ml)
olive or vegetable oil

2 teaspoons chopped
fresh oregano

1 tablespoon brandy

½ cup (4 fl oz/125 ml)
veal stock

oregano sprigs

❖ Dry the liver on kitchen paper. Place the flour in a plastic bag with salt and pepper to taste, then add a few slices of liver. Seal the bag and shake to coat each slice thinly and evenly. Remove liver from bag and shake off excess flour. Repeat with the remaining slices.

❖ Heat half the oil in a heavy pan over medium–high heat. Add a few slices of liver and cook very quickly until the surface is well seared and the meat is tender and slightly underdone. Remove from pan and keep warm while you cook the remaining liver, adding more oil as needed.

❖ Arrange on warmed serving plates and scatter on the oregano. Deglaze the pan with the brandy, add the stock, and boil briskly to reduce. Season to taste. Pour over the liver, garnish with oregano, and serve at once.

taipei chicken
with mixed greens

serves 4

2 cups (12 oz/375 g) shredded cooked
chicken, warmed

4 oz (125 g) packaged crisp chow mein noodles

1/4 cup (3/4 oz/20 g) thinly sliced green
(spring) onion

1/4 cup (2 fl oz/60 ml) soy sauce

2 tablespoons toasted (Asian) sesame oil

2 tablespoons rice wine vinegar

2 tablespoons water

2 teaspoons sugar

2 teaspoons peeled and grated fresh ginger

1 small fresh red or green chile (mild or hot,
according to taste), seeded and finely chopped

mixed fresh salad greens, to serve

❖ In a large mixing bowl, combine
the chicken, noodles, and green onion.

❖ In a small saucepan, combine the
soy sauce, sesame oil, vinegar, water,
sugar, ginger, and chile. Bring to a boil,
stirring to dissolve the sugar. Remove
from heat, allow to cool a little, and
pour over the chicken mixture. Toss
to mix. Serve atop mixed salad greens.

mexican chicken with salsa

This marvelous Mexican-inspired dish is good fare for a warm day—or any time. If tortillas are unavailable, substitute steamed rice.

1 small avocado

3 limes

1 small tomato, coarsely chopped

¼ cup (2 fl oz/60 ml) vegetable oil

½ cup (2 oz/60 g) chopped red (Spanish) onion

2 tablespoons chopped cilantro (fresh coriander), plus extra to garnish

salt and crushed dried chiles

2 boneless, skinless chicken breast halves

2 cloves garlic, cut in half

½ cup (4 fl oz/125 ml) chicken stock

1 head green lettuce, shredded, or 1 bunch arugula (rocket) leaves, washed and stemmed

8 corn tortillas, warmed

◈ To make the salsa, peel, pit, and coarsely chop the avocado. In a bowl, combine the avocado, the juice of 1 lime, the tomato, half of the oil, the onion, cilantro, and salt and crushed dried chiles to taste. Stir well and set aside.

◈ Cut the chicken breasts lengthwise into strips 1 inch (2.5 cm) wide and place in a bowl. Squeeze the juice of 1 lime over the chicken and toss gently.

◈ Warm the remaining oil in a large frying pan over medium-high heat. Add the garlic and sauté until soft, 1–2 minutes. Discard garlic. Add the chicken and sauté, turning the pieces as they become golden, about 1 minute on each side. Transfer to a warmed plate; keep warm in a low oven while you prepare the rest of the dish.

◈ Pour off the oil from the pan. Add the stock to the pan and bring to a boil over high heat. Deglaze the pan by stirring to dislodge any browned bits. Boil until the liquid is reduced by about one half. Season to taste with salt and crushed dried chiles.

◈ Arrange some lettuce or arugula on individual plates and top with some of the chicken strips. Pour the warm sauce over the chicken, then add some salsa to each plate.

◈ Cut the remaining lime into quarters. Garnish each plate with a lime quarter and a sprinkling of chopped cilantro. Serve with warmed tortillas.

beef and ginger stir-fry

serves 2–4

MARINADE

1 tablespoon light soy sauce

2 teaspoons cornstarch (cornflour)

1 teaspoon sugar

1 tablespoon peanut oil

6 oz (185 g) beef fillet, thinly sliced

SAUCE

1 tablespoon light soy sauce

1 tablespoon oyster sauce

½ cup (4 fl oz/125 ml) chicken stock

2 teaspoons cornstarch (cornflour)

1 teaspoon Chinese rice wine

1 cup (8 fl oz/250 ml) peanut oil

6–8 slices ginger, each ⅛ inch (3 mm) thick, thinly shredded

3 green (spring) onions, cut into 2-inch (5-cm) lengths

For the marinade, combine the soy sauce, cornstarch, sugar, and peanut oil in a bowl. Add the beef and turn to coat well. Marinate for 15 minutes.

For the sauce, in a separate bowl, combine the soy sauce, oyster sauce, chicken stock, cornstarch, and rice wine. Mix well.

Heat the oil in a wok or skillet. Add the beef and its marinade and fry for 5 seconds, stirring with chopsticks to separate the slices. Remove beef, drain, and set aside.

Drain all but 1–2 tablespoons of oil from the wok and reheat. Add the ginger and green onions and stir-fry for 10 seconds. Return the beef to the wok and add the sauce. Bring to a boil. Transfer immediately to a warmed platter and serve.

recipe hint

To slice beef or other meat paper-thin, as the Chinese do when preparing stir-fries, it is easiest if you first partially freeze the meat. Wrap it in plastic wrap and place in the freezer for about an hour. Remove the plastic wrap and use a very sharp knife to slice the meat as thinly as possible. Such wafer-thin slices need only seconds to cook and yield a very tender, succulent result.

stir-fried chicken
with ginger

serves 3–4

A salad of snow peas and orange segments makes a good accompaniment to this stir-fry, and almond cookies make the perfect ending to the meal.

4 boneless, skinless chicken breast halves

2 tablespoons vegetable oil

1 clove garlic

2 green (spring) onions, including tender green tops, thinly sliced lengthwise and then cut crosswise into 2-inch (5-cm) pieces

2 tablespoons peeled and chopped fresh ginger

1/4 teaspoon crushed dried chiles

1/2 cup (4 fl oz/125 ml) chicken stock

salt and ground black pepper

2 tablespoons chopped crystallized ginger (optional)

◈ Trim any excess fat from the chicken breasts. Place the breasts between 2 sheets of waxed paper and, using the flat side of a meat mallet, pound lightly until they are slightly flattened and of an even thickness. Cut the breast halves lengthwise into strips 1 inch (2.5 cm) wide.

◈ Warm the oil in a large frying pan over medium–high heat. Add the garlic and chicken and sauté, turning the chicken pieces as they become golden, about 1 minute on each side.

◈ Stir in the green onion, fresh ginger, and crushed dried chiles and sauté for 1–2 minutes. Add the chicken stock and bring to a boil. Deglaze the pan by stirring to dislodge any browned bits on the bottom of the pan, then reduce the heat slightly and simmer for 2–3 minutes. Season to taste with salt and pepper. Remove the garlic and discard.

◈ Transfer the chicken and onions to a warmed platter. Pour the sauce over the top. Garnish with the crystallized ginger, if desired.

quick and easy
seafood

mussels
with fresh herbs

½ cup (2½ oz/75 g) finely chopped golden (French) shallots

⅓ cup (½ oz/15 g) finely shredded fresh basil

4 tablespoons fresh tarragon leaves

⅓ cup (½ oz/15 g) chopped fresh chives

⅓ cup (½ oz/15 g) chopped fresh parsley

1½ cups (12 fl oz/375 ml) vinaigrette, homemade or purchased

4 lb (2 kg) mussels in the shell, well scrubbed and beards removed

1 cup (8 fl oz/250 ml) water

½ cup (3 oz/90 g) roasted, peeled, and sliced red bell peppers (capsicums)

❖ In a small bowl, combine the shallots, basil, tarragon, chives, parsley, and vinaigrette. Mix well and set aside.

❖ Discard any mussels that do not close to the touch. In a large saucepan, bring the water to a boil. Add the mussels, cover, and steam over high heat, stirring once or twice, until the shells open, 3–5 minutes.

❖ Drain the mussels; discard any that have not opened. Place in a large serving bowl or divide equally among smaller individual bowls. Scatter the bell peppers evenly over the top.

❖ Pour the vinaigrette-herb mixture over the mussels and bell peppers. Serve immediately or let cool and serve at room temperature.

shrimp
with fried garlic
and baked tomato

serves 4

Fresh shrimp, sautéed in
butter, garlic, and herbs, is a
classic bistro dish. In this
recipe, baked tomatoes give
the dish still more substance
and bright color. Vine-ripened
tomatoes provide the best
flavor. Serve with crusty
French bread to sop up all
the delicious juices.

4 tomatoes, about 1 1/2 lb (750 g) total weight

salt and ground black pepper

1/3 cup (3 fl oz/90 ml) olive oil

1 lb (500 g) medium-sized shrimp (prawns),
peeled and deveined

1 tablespoon finely chopped garlic

1 tablespoon sherry vinegar

2 tablespoons chopped fresh parsley

dash of cayenne pepper

◈ Preheat an oven to 450°F (230°C/Gas Mark 6).

◈ Cut the tomatoes in halves and place them, cut side up, in a shallow baking dish. Season to taste with salt and pepper and drizzle on 2 tablespoons of the olive oil. Bake until the tomatoes are cooked through but still firm, about 15 minutes.

◈ About 3 minutes before the tomatoes are done, in a frying pan over high heat, warm 1 tablespoon of the olive oil. Add the shrimp and salt and pepper to taste and sauté until the shrimp are pink and firm, 2–3 minutes.

◈ Transfer the baked tomatoes to individual serving dishes. Place the sautéed shrimp on top of the tomatoes, dividing them evenly.

◈ In a small saucepan over high heat, combine the garlic and the remaining 3 tablespoons olive oil, and sauté until the garlic turns golden brown, about 1 minute.

◈ Add the vinegar and deglaze the pan by stirring to dislodge any browned bits from the bottom of the pan, about 30 seconds. Immediately spoon the contents of the saucepan over the shrimp and tomatoes, dividing it evenly among the servings. Sprinkle with the parsley and cayenne. Serve at once.

sea scallops
with shaved fennel

serves 4

The faint aniseed flavor of fresh fennel adds a subtle complement to sautéed sea scallops in this simple dish. The key to this recipe is to slice the fennel paper-thin so that it appears "shaved." Use a mandoline or an extremely sharp knife for the desired effect. Serve this dish hot or at room temperature over a bed of hot white rice, if you like.

2 bulbs fennel

2 teaspoons salt

2 tablespoons olive oil

20 sea scallops, about 1 lb (500 g) total weight

1 cup (8 fl oz/250 ml) tomato pasta sauce

pinch of ground white pepper

$1/2$ teaspoon cayenne pepper

2 tablespoons chopped fresh parsley

❖ Remove and discard any bruised outer leaves from the fennel bulbs, then cut off any stalks and feathery tops. Using an electric slicer, a mandoline, or a very sharp knife, slice the fennel bulbs crosswise as thinly as possible. Place the fennel slices in a sieve or colander and sprinkle with 1 teaspoon of the salt, tossing the fennel to distribute evenly. Let stand for 30 minutes to drain off any water drawn out by the salt. Then rinse under cold running water and dry thoroughly with paper towels.

❖ In a large frying pan over high heat, warm the olive oil. Add the scallops and cook, turning once, until golden brown, 1–1½ minutes per side.

❖ Add the fennel and the tomato pasta sauce and stir well. Then stir in the remaining 1 teaspoon salt and the white and cayenne peppers. Bring to a boil and cook, stirring, until the scallops are firm to the touch, 1–2 minutes longer.

❖ Transfer to a warmed platter or individual plates and sprinkle with the chopped parsley. Serve at once.

serves 3–4 as an appetizer

36 oysters

LEMON VINAIGRETTE

½ cup (4 fl oz/125 ml) olive oil

3 tablespoons lemon juice

2 teaspoons grain mustard

1 teaspoon sugar

HORSERADISH CREAM SAUCE

1 cup (8 fl oz/250 ml) sour cream

*2 tablespoons freshly grated horseradish
or 1 tablespoon cream-style
prepared horseradish*

2 tablespoon capers, drained

2 drops hot-pepper sauce, such as Tabasco

CILANTRO PESTO WITH LIME AND CHILES

2 cloves garlic

2 mild green chiles, seeded

*1 cup (1 oz/30 g) cilantro (fresh coriander)
leaves, washed and dried*

2 tablespoons fresh lime juice

❖ For the lemon vinaigrette, combine all the ingredients in a screwtop jar and shake well.

❖ For the horseradish cream, mix all the ingredients until well combined. Refrigerate for at least 2 hours before serving.

❖ For the cilantro pesto, combine all the ingredients in a food processor and process until finely chopped, but still retaining some texture. Refrigerate for at least 1 hour before serving.

❖ Just before serving, shuck the oysters, taking care not to lose any of their flavorful juices. Arrange the oysters in their half-shells on a large platter. Place each of the dipping sauces in a separate small bowl and add to the platter. Serve immediately.

oysters
with dipping sauces

crisp fish pieces
with tartare sauce

serves 4 (or 8 as an appetizer)

TARTARE SAUCE

2 hard-cooked (hard-boiled) eggs

1 raw egg yolk

salt and ground white pepper

1 cup (8 fl oz/250 ml) vegetable oil

1 tablespoon white wine vinegar

1 teaspoon finely chopped parsley

1 teaspoon finely chopped capers

1 teaspoon finely chopped
dill pickle (gherkin)

1½ lb (750 g) fillets of thin white
fish such as halibut, turbot, or
sole, or small fillets of whiting

1½ cups (6 oz/185 g) all-purpose
(plain) flour

1 teaspoon salt

½ teaspoon white pepper

2 large eggs, beaten

2 cups (8 oz/250 g) fine dry
bread crumbs

vegetable oil, for deep-frying

lemon wedges, to serve

❖ For the sauce, remove the yolks from the hard-cooked eggs and press through a sieve into a mixing bowl. Add the raw egg yolk and beat until smooth, adding salt and pepper to taste. Slowly add the vegetable oil, whisking briskly, to make a thick, creamy emulsion. From time to time, add a few drops of the vinegar. When the mixture is emulsified and all the vinegar has been added, stir in the parsley, capers, and dill pickle. Spoon into a small serving dish.

❖ Cut the fish diagonally across the fillets into pieces ¾ inch (2 cm) wide. Combine the flour, salt, and pepper. Dip each piece of fish into the seasoned flour, then into the beaten egg, and finally into the bread crumbs to coat evenly. Chill for 30 minutes.

❖ Heat the deep-frying oil and fry the fish, a few pieces at a time, until crisp and golden. Drain on a rack covered with paper towels and serve hot with the tartare sauce and lemon wedges.

trout
wrapped in ham

serves 4

*4 freshwater trout,
cleaned with heads intact,
each about ¾ lb (375 g)*

*salt and ground
black pepper*

*8 thin slices cured ham,
such as serrano
or prosciutto*

*1 cup (5 oz/155 g)
all-purpose (plain) flour,
or as needed*

*⅓ cup (3 fl oz/80 ml)
olive oil*

lemon wedges

❖ Sprinkle the trout inside and out with salt and pepper to taste. Slip 1 slice of ham inside each trout. Wrap a second ham slice around the center of each trout, leaving the head and tail exposed. Skewer the cavity closed with toothpicks or tie the fish around the middle with kitchen string.

❖ In a large frying pan over medium heat, warm the olive oil. Spread the flour on a large plate. Dip the trout in the flour, coating it evenly. Fry, turning once, until golden on both sides, about 4 minutes per side. Transfer to a warmed platter or individual plates.

❖ Remove the toothpicks or string from the trout. Serve hot with lemon wedges.

grilled
swordfish kabobs

serves 4

½ cup (4 fl oz/125 ml)
olive oil

6 tablespoons (3 fl oz/90 ml)
fresh lemon juice

1 teaspoon paprika

2 bay leaves, crushed, plus
12 whole bay leaves

2 lb (1 kg) swordfish fillets,
cut into 1¼-inch (3-cm) cubes

2 lemons, thinly sliced, plus
lemon wedges for serving

2 green bell peppers
(capsicums), seeded,
deribbed, and cut into
1¼-inch (3-cm) squares

16 ripe but firm
cherry tomatoes

salt and ground
black pepper

❖ In a shallow nonaluminum bowl, whisk together the olive oil, lemon juice, paprika, and crushed bay leaves. Add the swordfish cubes, turning to coat well. Cover and marinate in the refrigerator for about 4 hours.

❖ Prepare a fire in a charcoal grill (barbecue) or preheat a broiler (griller).

❖ Remove the fish cubes from the marinade, reserving the marinade.

❖ Thread the cubes onto oiled metal skewers, alternating them with the whole bay leaves, lemon slices, bell peppers, and cherry tomatoes. Sprinkle with salt and pepper.

❖ Place the kabobs on an oiled grill rack or a broiler pan and grill or broil, turning as needed and basting a few times with the reserved marinade, until the fish is opaque throughout, about 10 minutes. Discard any unused marinade.

❖ Transfer the kabobs to a warmed platter and serve hot, accompanied with lemon wedges.

187

stir-fried shrimp
with shredded vegetables

serves 4

12 large uncooked shrimp (prawns)

1 medium onion

2 green (spring) onions

1 red bell pepper (capsicum), thinly sliced lengthwise

3 tablespoons vegetable oil

1 medium carrot, thinly sliced

3 thin slices fresh ginger, cut into fine shreds

12 snowpeas (mangetout)

½ cup (4 fl oz/125 ml) light chicken stock or water

1 tablespoon light or low-salt soy sauce

1 teaspoon cornstarch (cornflour)

salt and ground white pepper

hot cooked white rice, to serve

❖ Peel and devein the shrimp, leaving the last section of the shell and the tail intact. Cutting from top to base, slice the onion into narrow strips; separate the pieces. Cut the green onions into 1¾-inch (4-cm) lengths, then slice them lengthwise into fine shreds.

❖ In a wok or large frying pan, warm the oil. Add the onion, bell pepper, and carrot and stir-fry until beginning to soften, 3–4 minutes; transfer to a plate. Stir-fry the shrimp until they change color and are barely cooked through, 2–3 minutes; remove from the pan. Add the green onions, ginger, and snowpeas and stir-fry for 30 seconds. Return the shrimp and vegetables to the pan.

❖ Combine the stock, soy sauce, and cornstarch; add this mixture to the pan and stir over high heat until the sauce thickens. Season with salt and pepper to taste. Serve at once over white rice.

❖ NOTE: The vegetables can be cut up several hours in advance and stored in the refrigerator. Do not cook until just before serving time.

fish fillets
with lemon
and coriander seed

serves 6–8 as an appetizer
or 4 as a main course

This recipe relies on simplicity and the subtle marriage of complementary flavors for its success. The lightly spiced red bell pepper sauce makes an ideal partner for any type of firm, white fish fillet. It would also go well with chicken.

2 teaspoons coriander seeds

2 tablespoons fresh lemon juice

2 tablespoons water

¼ cup (1½ oz/45 g) roasted, peeled, and chopped red bell pepper (capsicum)

⅓ cup (3 fl oz/80 ml) olive oil

1 teaspoon salt, plus extra to taste

½ teaspoon ground white pepper, plus extra to taste

4 fillets of firm white fish, such as monkfish, sea bass, or cod, ¼ lb (125 g) each

2 tablespoons chopped fresh parsley

◈ In a blender, combine the coriander seeds, lemon juice, water, bell pepper, olive oil, the 1 teaspoon salt, and ½ teaspoon white pepper. Blend at high speed until smooth and creamy, about 1 minute. Pour the purée through a fine-mesh sieve into a clean bowl. Set aside.

◈ If using monkfish, trim off any thick outer membrane from the fillets. Sprinkle both sides of each fish fillet with salt and pepper to taste. Place on a steamer rack over (not touching) gently boiling water. Cover and steam until opaque throughout when pierced with a knife, 6–7 minutes.

◈ Transfer the fillets to warmed individual plates. Spoon the sauce evenly over the top and sides of the fish. Sprinkle with the parsley and serve at once.

swordfish
with spinach and
citrus vinaigrette

serves 4

These sautéed fish fillets
are served *à la florentine* (on
a bed of spinach)—a popular
way of preparing seafood
throughout France. This
recipe is distinguished by
its zesty vinaigrette, which
combines three types of
citrus with the pan juices.
The result is light yet
extremely flavorful.

¼ cup (2 fl oz/60 ml) water

¼ cup (2 oz/60 g) unsalted butter

⅓ cup (3 fl oz/80 ml) olive oil

1¼ lb (625 g) spinach leaves, stems removed,
leaves carefully washed

salt and ground black pepper

4 swordfish steaks, about 5 oz (155 g) each

juice of ½ orange

juice of ½ lemon

juice of ¼ grapefruit

¼ cup (2 fl oz/60 ml) veal stock or chicken stock

❖ In a large saucepan over high heat, combine the water, butter, and 2 tablespoons of the olive oil. Once the butter has melted completely, add the spinach leaves and salt and pepper to taste. Cover and cook, stirring every 20–30 seconds, until the spinach is wilted, about 2 minutes. Remove from the heat, cover, and set aside.

❖ In a large sauté pan over high heat, warm 1 tablespoon of the olive oil. Sprinkle both sides of the swordfish steaks with salt and pepper to taste. Place the swordfish steaks in the hot pan and cook, turning once, until done to your liking, 1–2 minutes on each side for medium-rare. Transfer the fish steaks to a plate and cover to keep warm.

❖ Pour off any oil remaining in the sauté pan and place over high heat. When the pan is hot, pour in the citrus juices and deglaze the pan by stirring to dislodge any browned bits from the bottom of the pan. Boil until the liquid is reduced by half, then add the veal or chicken stock and salt and pepper to taste. Return to a boil and stir in the remaining 2 tablespoons olive oil. Remove from the heat.

❖ Drain the spinach in a sieve and divide equally among warmed individual plates. Place the swordfish steaks on top of the spinach and spoon the citrus mixture evenly over the steaks. Serve immediately.

quick-bake rice

serves 4–6

The rice can be made ahead of time and frozen, or assembled up to 12 hours ahead and refrigerated until needed. If longer advance preparation is required, omit the shrimp.

1½ cups (10 oz/315 g) long-grain white rice

3 cups (24 fl oz/750 ml) water

10 oz (300 g) package frozen spinach

1 large onion, sliced

¼ cup (2 oz/60 g) butter

1 clove garlic, chopped

salt and ground black pepper

grated nutmeg

5 oz (155 g) peeled, cooked small shrimp

2 tablespoons pine nuts, toasted

◈ Preheat oven to 375°F (190°C/Gas Mark 5).

◈ Place the rice in a heavy saucepan with a tightly fitting lid. Add the water and bring to a boil. Cover, reduce heat to very low, and cook gently for 12 minutes. (If the saucepan lid does not fit tightly, cover the pan with a double layer of aluminum foil before placing the lid on.)

◈ Meanwhile, thaw the spinach in a microwave oven or covered saucepan over gentle heat. In a small pan, sauté the onion in half the butter until golden brown. Add the garlic and sauté briefly, then add the spinach and cook briefly. Add salt, pepper, and nutmeg to taste.

◈ Use some of the remaining butter to thickly grease a casserole or rice mold. Mix the shrimp with half the rice. Mix the pine nuts with the remainder. Place the pine nut rice in the bottom of the prepared dish, spread the spinach mixture on top, and cover with the shrimp rice. Cut any remaining butter into small cubes and place on top. Bake for 12 minutes.

◈ Invert onto a serving plate and garnish with sprigs of fresh herbs.

tea-smoked shrimp

This recipe uses a simple method of home smoking to impart a distinctive Asian-inspired flavor to the shrimp.

16 large raw shrimp (prawns) in their shells

1/2 teaspoon salt

2 teaspoons ginger juice (use a garlic press) or ginger wine

3 tablespoons jasmine tea leaves

4 pieces Chinese dried orange zest

1 tablespoon sugar

1 small fresh mango, peeled, pit removed

2 teaspoons sweet chile sauce (or to taste)

1 teaspoon finely chopped fresh basil

1 large ripe avocado, peeled, pitted, and thinly sliced

sprigs of fresh basil

◈ Rinse and dry the shrimp. Use a sharp knife to cut through the shell along the center back. Lift out the dark vein and discard. Sprinkle the shrimp along the cut area with the salt and ginger juice or wine.

◈ Fold a double thickness of aluminum foil into a 7-inch (18-cm) square and place inside a large wok. Place the tea leaves, orange zest, and sugar on the foil and position a metal rack over them. Arrange the shrimp on the rack. Cover with the lid and place over high heat. When the contents begin to smoke, the heat may be reduced. Smoke-cook until the shrimp are firm and cooked through but have not begun to dry out, about 12 minutes (the cooking time will depend on the size of the shrimp). Remove from the wok. Remove heads and shells. Arrange four shrimp in fan shapes on each of four large warmed serving plates.

◈ Meanwhile, purée the mango in a food processor or blender and stir in the chile sauce and basil. Place a spoonful of the sauce on each plate, garnish with avocado slices and basil sprigs, and serve at once.

cod poached in coconut milk

serves 6

2–2½ lb (1–1.25 kg) cod or
other thick white fish fillets

1 large onion, sliced

1½ tablespoons vegetable oil

2 stalks lemongrass

1 fresh red chile, seeded

3 cups (24 fl oz/750 ml)
thick coconut milk

2 tablespoons light soy sauce
or Thai fish sauce

salt

ground white pepper

hot cooked rice, to serve

✧ Cut the fish into 2-inch (5-cm) squares and place in a medium saucepan.

✧ In a frying pan over medium–high heat, sauté the onion in the oil until well colored; add to the fish. Cut the lemongrass stalks into 4-inch (10-cm) lengths and slit in halves lengthwise. Add lemongrass and all of the remaining ingredients to the fish and cook over moderate heat for about 10 minutes, or until the fish is just cooked through. Do not overcook. Serve with steamed rice, either plain or flavored with turmeric, salt, and chopped garlic.

✧ NOTE: Cracked crabs or whole peeled shrimp (prawns) are both delicious cooked this way.

sardines
with garlic oil

serves 4

12 fresh sardines

1 1/2 teaspoons coarse salt

3 tablespoons vegetable oil
or olive oil

3–4 garlic cloves, finely
chopped

fresh herbs of your choice, such
as dill, Italian (flat-leaf) parsley,
or cilantro (fresh coriander)

lemon slices, to serve

✥ Sprinkle the sardines with salt about 20 minutes before cooking.

✥ Brush lightly with oil and cook on a grill (barbecue) rack or under the broiler (griller), turning once, until just done, 8–10 minutes total.

✥ Meanwhile, in a small pan, heat the remaining oil and add the garlic. Pour the hot garlic oil over the fish and serve at once, garnished with the herbs and lemon.

sea perch
with herb butter

serves 4

2 lemons

4 sea perch fillets

¼ cup (2 oz/60 g) butter

½ teaspoon salt

⅓ teaspoon black pepper

2 teaspoons minced parsley

1 teaspoon chopped dill

1 teaspoon chopped chives

1 tablespoon minced red bell pepper (capsicum)

1 clove garlic, finely chopped

4 small zucchini (courgettes)

hot cooked white rice, to serve

dill sprigs, to serve

❖ Cut one lemon in halves and squeeze one half over the fish. Cut the remaining half into 2 wedges and the other lemon into 4 wedges and set aside. Mash the butter with the salt, pepper, herbs, bell pepper, and garlic. Spread over the fish and pan-fry until cooked through, turning once.

❖ Slice the zucchini lengthwise without cutting through the stalk end. Drop into boiling, lightly salted water and simmer until just tender. Drain well. Arrange one zucchini in a fan shape on each of four warmed serving plates. Place one fish fillet on each plate, along with cooked rice, lemon wedges, and dill sprigs. Spoon any sauce left in the pan over the fish. Serve at once.

fish, asparagus, and pea casserole

serves 6

2 lb (1 kg) cod or
other thick white fish fillets

1 cup (8 fl oz/250 ml)
dry white wine

1 bunch thin green asparagus

1 cup (6 oz/185 g) green peas

salt and ground white pepper

1 cup (8 fl oz/250 ml)
light (single) cream

2 teaspoons chopped fresh
dill or parsley

1 cup (6 oz/185 g) canned or
fresh shelled clams (optional)

boiled potatoes or hot cooked
rice, to serve

❖ Cut the fish into 2-inch (5-cm) pieces and place in a flameproof casserole. Add the wine, cover the pan, and simmer gently for 6 minutes.

❖ Meanwhile, cut the asparagus into 2-inch (4-cm) lengths. Boil in lightly salted water for 4 minutes; drain.

❖ Boil the peas in lightly salted water until almost tender; drain.

❖ Add the asparagus and the peas to the casserole along with salt and pepper to taste and the cream. Simmer the mixture gently for 3–4 minutes, then add the chopped herbs and clams, if using.

❖ Serve with boiled potatoes or rice.

grilled shrimp
with mango salsa

serves 4–6

1 cup (8 fl oz/250 ml) olive oil

8 cloves garlic, thinly sliced

juice of 2 limes

1 teaspoon salt

½ teaspoon ground black pepper

2 lb (1 kg) large shrimp (prawns), peeled and deveined (20–24 shrimp)

MANGO SALSA

2 ripe mangoes

6 green (spring) onions, including tender green tops, thinly sliced

2 fresh jalapeño chiles, stemmed, seeded (if desired), and finely diced

¼ cup (¼ oz/7 g) coarsely chopped cilantro (fresh coriander)

juice of 2 limes

1 teaspoon salt

lime wedges, to serve (optional)

◈ In a frying pan over medium heat, warm the olive oil. Add the garlic and cook, stirring occasionally, until soft, 3–5 minutes. Remove from the heat, pour into a shallow nonaluminum dish, and let cool. Add the lime juice, salt, and pepper. Mix well.

◈ Using bamboo skewers that have been soaked in cold water for at least 1 hour, thread 4 or 5 shrimp onto each skewer, passing the skewer through points near both the head and tail sections of each shrimp. Place the skewers in the olive oil mixture, turning to coat evenly. Cover and let marinate in the refrigerator for at least 2 hours or up to 12 hours.

◈ To make the salsa, peel each mango and cut the flesh from the pit. Cut into $\frac{1}{4}$-inch (6-mm) dice and place in a bowl. Add the green onion, chile, cilantro, lime juice, and salt. Stir to mix, cover, and refrigerate for at least 30 minutes before serving.

◈ Prepare a fire in a charcoal grill (barbecue) or preheat a broiler (griller).

◈ Remove the shrimp from the marinade, reserving the marinade. Place the skewers on the grill rack or under the broiler, about 3 inches (7.5 cm) from the heat, and cook, turning and basting with marinade once, until the shrimp turn pink and are opaque throughout, about 3 minutes per side. Discard remaining marinade.

◈ To serve, arrange a bed of salsa on each plate and top with a skewer of shrimp, or remove the shrimp from each skewer and arrange atop the salsa.

◈ Garnish with lime wedges, if desired, and serve hot.

spicy grilled
snapper
with dill

1 or 2 snapper or bream
(about 2 lb/1 kg total weight)

salt and ground black pepper

2 tablespoons melted butter,
olive oil, or vegetable oil

1 lemon, sliced

3–4 fresh dill sprigs

❖ Prepare a fire in a charcoal grill (barbecue) or preheat a broiler (griller).

❖ Clean the fish and make several diagonal slashes on each side. Season inside and out with salt and pepper. On a piece of aluminum foil large enough to enclose the fish, brush the butter or oil over an area the same size as the fish and place the fish on it. Place several lemon slices and a sprig or two of dill in the cavity of the fish and arrange the remaining lemon and herbs over the fish. Wrap the foil around the fish, folding the edges over to seal.

❖ Grill or broil over moderate heat until tender, about 25 minutes for one large fish and 15 for two smaller fish. Test by inserting a skewer into the thickest part; if the flesh is tender and white, the fish is done.

thai grilled caramelized fish

4 whole fillets of white
flatfish, such as plaice, sole,
or flounder, skinned

1 teaspoon salt

juice of 2 limes

1/3 cup (2 1/2 oz/75 g) firmly
packed brown sugar

lime wedges, to serve

❖ Preheat a broiler (griller).

❖ Halve each fillet lengthwise, sprinkle with the salt
and lime juice, roll up, and secure with toothpicks. Set
aside for 20–25 minutes. Before broiling, rub all over
with the sugar.

❖ Broil (grill) the fish until cooked and caramelized,
4–5 minutes each side.

❖ Remove the toothpicks. Serve with lime wedges.

marinated trout
with olives and chile

serves 8

½ cup (4 fl oz/125 ml) olive oil

¾ cup (6 fl oz/185 ml) coconut milk

¼ cup (2 fl oz/60 ml) lime juice

2 hot red chiles, chopped

½ cup (3 oz/90 g) stuffed olives, chopped

1 onion, chopped

¼ cup (¼ oz/7 g) chopped mint leaves

2 limes, sliced

8 small trout, cleaned

❖ Combine the oil, coconut milk, lime juice, chiles, olives, onion, and mint in a shallow dish. Add the lime slices and trout, cover, and marinate in the refrigerator for at least 4 hours.

❖ Prepare a fire in a charcoal grill (barbecue) or preheat a broiler (griller).

❖ Wrap each fish in aluminum foil, adding a slice of lime and 2 tablespoons of the marinade. Grill (barbecue) or broil (grill), turning once, until the fish is cooked through, about 8 minutes on each side.

❖ Arrange the fish on warmed serving plates and serve at once.

shrimp
with fresh herbs

serves 6

1 lb (1 kg) medium shrimp
(prawns), peeled and deveined

1 clove garlic, crushed

1/4 cup (2 fl oz/60 ml) olive oil

salt and ground black pepper

1 1/2 oz (45 g) fresh
flat-leaf (Italian) parsley

1 1/2 oz (45 g) fresh marjoram

1 1/2 oz (45 g) fresh thyme

1 1/2 oz (45 g) fresh tarragon

1 1/2 oz (45 g) fresh basil

1/4 cup (2 fl oz/60 ml)
dry white wine

❖ Wash the shrimp and dry well.

❖ Finely chop most of the herbs, reserving a few whole leaves of each for garnish.

❖ Over medium heat, fry the garlic gently in the oil until golden brown, then remove it. Add the shrimp to the oil and cook, stirring, until they begin to turn pink and curl up, about 2 minutes. Season with salt and pepper to taste, then stir in the chopped herbs and wine. Cook for 1–2 minutes longer, then serve immediately, garnished with the reserved herbs.

fresh
tuna niçoise

1 small cucumber, about 8 oz (250 g)

1 bunch green (spring) onions, trimmed

2 oz (60 g) pitted black olives

8 oz (250 g) cherry tomatoes, halved

1 lb (500 g) fine green beans

DRESSING

10 fl oz (300 ml) tomato juice

1 tablespoon balsamic vinegar

2 tablespoons lemon juice

2 tablespoons soy sauce

4 tablespoons olive oil

2 tablespoons honey

2 cloves garlic, crushed

salt and pepper

6 tuna steaks, about 6 oz (180 g) each

3 hard-cooked (hard-boiled) eggs, shelled and quartered

❖ Cut the cucumber in half lengthwise and remove the seeds. Slice the flesh into diagonal chunks. Slice the spring onions in half lengthwise and cut into similar-size pieces. Place both in a bowl with the olives and cherry tomatoes.

❖ Top, tail, and halve the green beans and plunge into boiling water for 3 minutes. Lift out with a slotted spoon and place in a bowl of ice-cold water for a few minutes to refresh. Drain well. Mix thoroughly with the other vegetables, cover, and place in the refrigerator.

❖ To make the dressing, whisk together the tomato juice, vinegar, lemon juice, soy sauce, olive oil, and honey. Add the garlic and salt and pepper to taste.

❖ Preheat a broiler (griller).

❖ Brush each tuna steak with some of the dressing, coating both sides well. Broil (grill) until the steaks are golden and feel firm to the touch, about 5 minutes each side.

❖ Toss the vegetables in a little of the dressing and divide equally among individual serving plates. Add the eggs. Top each serving with a tuna steak. Serve extra dressing separately.

salmon and pesto parcels

serves 2

2 tablespoons butter, melted

2 teaspoons pesto sauce

2½ fl oz (75 ml) fromage frais or low-fat soft cheese

2 sheets filo pastry, each about 12 x 18 inches (30 x 45 cm)

2 salmon fillets, each about 4 oz (125 g), skinned

2 oz (60 g) button mushrooms, wiped and sliced

salt and ground black pepper

salad leaves, to serve

❖ Preheat an oven to 200°C (400°F/Gas Mark 6). Lightly brush a baking sheet with some of the melted butter.

❖ Mix the pesto with the fromage frais or soft cheese.

❖ Halve each sheet of filo pastry. Brush each half with melted butter, then put one piece atop another, buttered sides up, to make two rectangles.

❖ Place a salmon fillet in the centre of each pastry rectangle. Top with the mushrooms and half of the pesto sauce mixture, then sprinkle with salt and pepper to taste. Wrap the pastry around to enclose the fish. Brush with the remaining butter. Place on the prepared baking sheet.

❖ Bake until well browned, about 15 minutes. To serve, open the pastry and spoon in the remaining pesto sauce mixture. Serve hot, accompanied with salad leaves.

lemon sole
with salsa verde

serves 6

2 bunches of fresh basil
(about 2 large handfuls),
chopped

2 cloves garlic, skinned
and crushed

4 oz (125 g) grated Parmesan
cheese

4 hard-cooked (hard-boiled)
eggs, chopped

olive oil

salt and pepper

12 lemon sole fillets, skinned

flat-leaf (Italian) parsley,
to garnish

❖ Preheat a broiler (griller).

❖ To make the salsa verde, mix the basil with the garlic, Parmesan, and hard-cooked eggs. Add enough oil so that the mixture is moist yet still stiff enough to hold its shape. Add salt and pepper to taste.

❖ Spread each sole fillet out on a board. Season with salt and pepper, brush with oil, and broil (grill), turning once, until cooked, 8–10 minutes.

❖ To serve, place two of the fillets on each of six warmed serving plates. With two spoons, make lozenge shapes with the salsa verde and arrange beside the fish. Garnish with parsley and serve at once.

quick and easy
vegetables
and grains

artichokes
with bacon

⅓ cup (3 oz/90 g) butter

2 leeks, washed, dried, and sliced,
or 2 onions, peeled and sliced

2 tablespoons chopped capers

2 tablespoons chopped anchovies

1 lb (500 g) canned artichoke hearts, drained

½ cup (4 fl oz/125 ml) dry white wine

1 garlic clove, crushed

1 cup (8 fl oz/250 ml) light (single) cream,
mixed with 2 teaspoons cornstarch (cornflour)

1 tablespoon olive or safflower oil

6 slices (rashers) bacon

2 tablespoons chopped fresh dill,
or 2 teaspoons dried dill

1 tablespoon chopped parsley

❖ Melt the butter in a nonaluminum pan, add leeks, and cook over low heat for 5 minutes, or until leeks soften. Add capers, anchovies, artichokes, wine, and garlic. Bring to a boil, reduce heat, and simmer for 3 minutes.

❖ Add the combined cream and cornstarch and stir until the mixture boils and thickens; remove from heat.

❖ Heat the oil in a frying pan, fry the bacon until crisp, then roughly chop. Add bacon, dill, and parsley to the leek mixture and stir over a low heat until heated through. Serve at once.

sautéed mushrooms with garlic

serves 4

Savor these garlicky sautéed mushrooms hot from the pan. Spoon them over toast as a snack, or alongside grilled lamb, beef, or chicken as a flavorful side dish. For a particularly delicious variation, combine chanterelles, portobellos, and cremini with the more common white mushrooms.

5 tablespoons (2 1/2 fl oz/75 ml) olive oil, or equal parts unsalted butter and olive oil

2 tablespoons minced garlic

1/4 cup (1 1/2 oz/45 g) diced bacon or cooked diced ham

1 lb (500 g) fresh mushrooms (see note), brushed clean and halved if small, or sliced 1/4 inch (6 mm) thick

1/2 cup (2 fl oz/60 ml) dry white wine or dry sherry, if needed

1/3 cup (1/2 oz/15 g) chopped fresh flat-leaf (Italian) parsley, or 1/4 cup (1/3 oz/10 g) chopped fresh flat-leaf (Italian) parsley and 2 tablespoons chopped fresh thyme

salt and ground black pepper

In a large frying pan over medium heat, warm the olive oil or melt the butter with the olive oil. Add the garlic and bacon or ham and sauté for 2 minutes. Raise the heat to high, add the mushrooms, and continue to sauté, stirring briskly, until they release their juices and the liquid evaporates, 5–8 minutes.

If the mushrooms do not release much liquid, add the wine or sherry and cook until the liquid evaporates.

Add the parsley (and thyme, if using) and stir well. Season to taste with salt and pepper and serve hot.

recipe hint

Garlic cloves tend to stick to the knife blade when you chop them, but this can be prevented by first sprinkling them with a little salt. Just remember to reduce or omit the amount of salt used in the rest of the dish.

Garlic cloves that have begun to shoot may be bitter. If you see a green shoot beginning to emerge, halve the clove and remove it.

indian
spiced rice

serves 6

3 tablespoons ghee or butter

2 cups (10 oz/315 g) long-grain white rice

1 teaspoon salt

1½ teaspoons garam masala

½ cup (3 oz/90 g) dried mixed fruit

¼ cup (2 oz/60 g) finely chopped dried apricots

2 whole cloves

seeds from 2 cardamom pods

1 cinnamon stick

2¾ cups (22 fl oz/685 ml) water

❖ In a medium saucepan with a heavy base and close-fitting lid, melt the ghee or butter. Add the rice and stir for 2–3 minutes. Add the remaining ingredients, stir well, and bring just to a boil. Reduce heat to the lowest setting, cover, and cook until light and fluffy, about 18 minutes. Stir with a fork to separate the grains. Discard the cloves and cinnamon stick. Serve hot.

❖ NOTE: This dish can be prepared ahead of time and reheated in the microwave oven on medium–high. This recipe can also be frozen—thaw in the refrigerator or on low in the microwave oven, then cover and reheat in the microwave or in a conventional oven.

asparagus
with olive oil
and parmesan

serves 4

2 bunches (1½ lb/750 g)
asparagus, trimmed

⅓ cup (3 fl oz/90 ml) olive oil,
plus extra to serve

6 oz (185 g) Parmesan cheese,
shaved, plus extra to serve

ground black pepper

◇ Steam or microwave the asparagus until tender.

◇ Place on a large platter, drizzle with the olive oil,
and sprinkle with the Parmesan and pepper to taste.

◇ Serve with extra Parmesan, pepper, and olive oil.

macaroni gratin
with wild mushrooms

serves 4–6

If you can't find good-quality wild mushrooms for this recipe, substitute 9 ounces (270 g) assorted dried ones. Reconstitute dried mushrooms in cold water to cover for a few hours, then drain well and squeeze out any excess liquid before using.

1½ cups (5 oz/150 g) dried elbow macaroni

2 tablespoons olive oil

2 tablespoons chopped golden (French) shallots

5 oz (150 g) fresh chanterelle mushrooms, brushed clean and trimmed

4 oz (125 g) fresh shiitake mushrooms, brushed clean and trimmed

2 oz (60 g) fresh oyster mushrooms, brushed clean and trimmed

salt and ground black pepper

1 tablespoon chopped fresh chives

1 tablespoon chopped fresh parsley

2 cups (8 oz/250 g) finely shredded Swiss cheese

❖ Preheat a broiler (griller).

❖ Fill a large saucepan three-fourths full of water and bring to a boil. Add the macaroni and return to a boil. Cook the macaroni until slightly tender to the bite, about 5 minutes.

❖ Meanwhile, in a large frying pan over medium–low heat, warm the olive oil. Add the shallots and sauté until translucent, about 2 minutes.

❖ Cut any large mushrooms in halves. Add all the mushrooms and salt and pepper to taste to the frying pan and sauté over medium heat until the mushrooms are soft and slightly browned, 4–5 minutes.

❖ When the pasta is done, drain it immediately and add it to the frying pan. Add the chives and parsley and stir to mix. Taste and adjust the seasoning.

❖ Transfer the mixture to a flameproof 9-inch (23-cm) gratin dish with 2-inch (5-cm) sides or individual gratin dishes. Sprinkle the Swiss cheese evenly over the top.

❖ Place under the broiler just until the cheese melts, about 2 minutes. Serve immediately.

broccoli
with lemon and herbs

1 lb (500 g) broccoli

½ cup (4 oz/125 g) butter

2 tablespoons lemon juice

2 tablespoons chopped fresh herbs such as parsley, oregano, thyme, and/or basil

salt and ground black pepper

❖ Cut the broccoli into florets. Steam or microwave until tender.

❖ Melt the butter in a small saucepan. Add the lemon juice, chopped herbs, and salt and pepper to taste.

❖ Pour the butter mixture over the broccoli, toss well, and serve immediately as an accompaniment to meat, poultry, or fish.

peas with ham and onions

8 green (spring) onions
or baby onions

4 cloves garlic

8 oz (250 g) sugar snap peas

8 oz (250 g) snow peas
(mangetout)

1 tablespoon olive oil

2 slices cooked ham, chopped

❖ Place the green onions and garlic in cold water. Bring to a boil and boil gently for 1 minute. Drain and remove the skins. Chop garlic and onions into pieces.

❖ Bring a pot of water to a boil, add the sugar snap peas, and cook for 30 seconds. Add the snow peas and cook for another 30 seconds. Drain.

❖ Heat the oil in a frying pan. Add the ham, green onions, and garlic. Sauté for 2 minutes. Add the peas, toss well, and serve immediately.

cauliflower
gratin

serves 6

1½ lb (750 g) cauliflower,
trimmed and cut
into large florets

1 cup (8 oz/250 g)
cottage cheese

½ cup (4 fl oz/125 ml) milk

¼ cup (2 fl oz/60 ml)
light sour cream

¼ cup (1 oz/30 g) freshly
grated Parmesan cheese

¼ cup (¼ oz/8 g) tightly
packed basil leaves

1 clove garlic

◈ Preheat a broiler (griller).

◈ Bring a large pan of salted water to a boil. Add the
cauliflower, return to a boil, and cook for 5 minutes,
or until tender. Drain and place in a lightly greased
flameproof casserole.

◈ Place the remaining ingredients in the bowl of a
food processor fitted with the metal blade and blend
until smooth. Heat gently until just warm, then pour
over the hot cauliflower. Place under the broiler and
broil (grill) until the top is just beginning to brown,
about 2 minutes. Serve immediately.

crisp
potato cakes

serves 2

3 potatoes, peeled and
finely shredded

1 egg yolk

1 tablespoon all-purpose
(plain) flour

oil, for frying

❖ Combine potatoes, egg yolk, and flour in a bowl.
Mix well.

❖ Divide the potato mixture into 4 portions and shape
each portion into a round. Fry the rounds in hot oil,
pressing down with a spatula to maintain the shape
and turning once, until the potato is golden brown
on both sides, about 10 minutes in total.

❖ Drain on paper towels and serve hot.

**serves 8 as an appetizer
or 4 as a side dish**

*1 lb (500 g) small zucchini
(courgettes), coarsely grated*

salt

*½ lb (250 g) feta cheese,
or equal parts feta and kasseri
or ricotta*

6 green (spring) onions, minced

*½ cup (½ oz/15 g) chopped
fresh dill*

*¼ cup (⅓ oz/10 g) chopped
fresh mint*

*¼ cup (⅓ oz/10 g) chopped
fresh flat-leaf (Italian) parsley*

3 eggs, lightly beaten

*1 cup (5 oz/155 g) all-purpose
(plain) flour*

salt and ground black pepper

peanut oil, for frying

*purchased or homemade
tzatziki, to serve (optional)*

❖ Place the zucchini in a sieve or colander, salt it lightly, and toss to mix. Let stand for 30 minutes to draw out the excess moisture. Using a kitchen towel, squeeze the zucchini dry and place it in a bowl. Crumble the cheese over the zucchini and add the green onion, dill, mint, parsley, eggs, flour, and salt and pepper to taste. Stir to mix well.

❖ In a deep frying pan over medium-high heat, pour in the peanut oil to a depth of ¼ inch (6 mm). When the oil is hot, using a serving spoon, drop spoonfuls of the batter into the oil, being careful not to crowd the pan. Fry, turning once, until nicely browned on both sides, 2–3 minutes per side. Using a slotted spoon or spatula, transfer the fritters to paper towels to drain. Keep warm in a low oven until all the fritters are cooked.

❖ Arrange the fritters on a warmed platter and serve hot, accompanied with tzatziki, if desired.

zucchini fritters

potatoes o'brien

serves 6

1½ tablespoons
butter, or as needed

1½ tablespoons
olive oil, or as needed

1 large yellow onion,
finely chopped

½ small red bell
pepper (capsicum),
seeded, deribbed,
and finely diced

½ small green bell
pepper (capsicum),
seeded, deribbed,
and finely diced

2 lb (1 kg) small white
or red potatoes,
peeled and cut into
½-inch (12-mm) cubes

salt and ground black
pepper

2 tablespoons finely
chopped fresh flat-leaf
(Italian) parsley

❖ In a large frying pan over medium-high heat, melt ½ tablespoon of the butter with ½ tablespoon of the olive oil. Add the onion and sauté, stirring occasionally, until golden brown and beginning to caramelize, 5–7 minutes. Do not allow the onion to scorch. Add the red and green bell peppers and sauté until beginning to soften, 3–5 minutes longer. Transfer to a large bowl and set aside.

❖ Add ½ tablespoon each of the remaining butter and olive oil to the same pan. Add half of the potatoes and cook, turning to brown on all sides, 5–7 minutes. If they become too dry, add a little more butter or oil. Transfer the browned potatoes to the bowl holding the pepper mixture. Repeat with the remaining butter, oil, and potatoes.

❖ Return all of the vegetables to the pan. Raise the heat to high so that the mixture quickly warms through. Remove from heat and season to taste with salt and pepper. Stir in the parsley. Transfer to a serving bowl and serve immediately.

asian stir-fry

serves 4

*1 bunch asparagus,
sliced diagonally*

*6½ oz (200 g) baby squash,
quartered*

1 tablespoon vegetable oil

2 teaspoons Asian sesame oil

*2 tablespoons peeled and grated
fresh ginger*

2 cloves garlic, finely chopped

*6½ oz (200 g) button mushrooms
(champignons), cut in half*

6½ oz (200 g) sugar snap peas

*3½ oz (100 g) snow peas
(mangetout)*

4 oz (125 g) soy bean shoots

*6½ oz (200 g) snowpea
(mangetout) sprouts*

1 tablespoon soy sauce

ground black pepper

❖ Blanch the asparagus and squash in boiling water. Refresh under cold water; drain well.

❖ In a large frying pan or wok over medium-high heat, warm the oils. Add the ginger and garlic and cook, stirring, for 30 seconds. Add the other vegetables in the order given, stirring and tossing continuously until crisp-tender, 4–5 minutes. Season with soy sauce and pepper to taste and serve immediately.

moroccan vegetable couscous

serves 6 as a side dish

1 tablespoon olive oil

½ cup (2 oz/60 g) chopped onion

½ cup (2½ oz/75 g) chopped red or green bell pepper (capsicum)

¼ cup (1¼ oz/40 g) finely diced carrot

¼ cup (1¼ oz/40 g) finely diced zucchini (courgette)

1 cup (8 fl oz/250 ml) chicken stock

1⅔ cups (5 oz/155 g) shredded cabbage

1 cup (6 oz/185 g) chopped tomato (2 medium)

1 tablespoon finely chopped cilantro (fresh coriander) or flat-leaf (Italian) parsley

¼ teaspoon salt

¼ teaspoon ground cardamom

¼ teaspoon caraway seed

⅛ teaspoon ground turmeric

⅔ cup (4 oz/125 g) quick-cooking couscous

❖ In a medium saucepan over medium heat, warm the olive oil. Add the onion, bell pepper, carrot, and zucchini and cook, stirring, until softened, about 5 minutes. Stir in the stock, cabbage, tomatoes, cilantro or parsley, salt, cardamom, caraway, and turmeric. Bring to a boil, then reduce heat, cover, and simmer for 10 minutes.

❖ Stir in the couscous. Remove from the heat, cover the pan again, and let stand for 5 minutes. Uncover, fluff with a fork, and serve immediately.

231

tempura vegetables
with dipping sauce

serves 12 as an appetizer

DIPPING SAUCE

3 tablespoons soy sauce

2 tablespoons orange juice

2 tablespoons dry sherry

*1 tablespoon finely chopped green
(spring) onion*

1 teaspoon sugar

1 teaspoon sesame seeds

*few splashes bottled hot-pepper sauce,
such as Tabasco, or to taste*

TEMPURA

*1½ cups (7 oz/220 g) all-purpose
(plain) flour*

*¼ teaspoon baking soda (bicarbonate
of soda)*

⅛ teaspoon salt

1 egg yolk, beaten

1¾ cups (13 fl oz/410 ml) ice water

*peanut oil or vegetable oil,
for deep-frying*

*1 lb (500 g) cut-up mixed fresh
vegetables, such as 1-inch (2.5-cm)
pieces of asparagus, green beans, or
Chinese long beans; sliced peeled
carrots, sweet or white potatoes,
or parsnips; broccoli florets; halved
mushrooms; sliced zucchini (courgettes)
or slender eggplants (aubergines);
and/or bell pepper (capsicum) strips*

tempura vegetables with dipping sauce

❖ To minimize the spattering when making tempura, be sure the vegetables are dry before you coat them in batter. Fry only a few pieces at a time to prevent them from sticking together.

❖ For the dipping sauce, in a small mixing bowl, combine the soy sauce, orange juice, sherry, green onion, sugar, sesame seeds, and hot-pepper sauce. Set aside.

❖ For the tempura, in a medium mixing bowl, stir together the flour, baking soda, and salt. Make a well in the center. Stir together the egg yolk and ice water, add all at once to the flour mixture, and stir just until combined (a few lumps should remain).

❖ In a deep, heavy saucepan or deep-fryer, pour in 2–3 inches (5–7.5 cm) of oil. Heat to 365°F (185°C) on a deep-frying thermometer.

❖ Dip the completely dry vegetables into the batter, a few pieces at a time, swirling to coat. Fry a few pieces at a time in the hot oil until golden, 2–3 minutes, turning once. Using a wire skimmer or slotted spoon, remove the vegetables from the oil and transfer to a wok rack or paper towels to drain. Keep warm in a low oven while you fry the remaining pieces in the same way. Serve warm with the dipping sauce.

squash fritters
with cilantro pesto

CILANTRO PESTO

2 bunches cilantro (fresh coriander)

½ cup (2½ oz/75 g) pumpkin seeds (pepitas)

2 cloves garlic, chopped

2 tablespoons lime juice

½ cup (4 fl oz/125 ml) olive oil

½ cup (2 oz/60 g) grated Parmesan cheese

1 lb (500 g) butternut squash

½ cup (2 oz/60 g) self-rising flour

1 teaspoon baking powder

1 egg

1 tablespoon olive oil

⅔ cup (5 fl oz/150 ml) water

vegetable oil, for shallow-frying

❖ For the pesto, remove leaves from cilantro stems. Discard stems. In a food processor, process leaves, pumpkin seeds, garlic, lime juice, and oil for 20 seconds. Scrape down sides of bowl and process for another 10 seconds. Stir in the Parmesan.

❖ Peel the squash and remove the seeds. Cut into slices ½ inch (1 cm) thick. Pat dry on paper towels.

❖ Combine flour and baking powder in a bowl. Beat in the egg, oil, and water, adding a little extra water if batter is too thick. Dip squash slices in the batter and shallow-fry in hot oil until golden. Serve with the pesto.

baked
tomatoes
with thyme

serves 4

8 medium tomatoes

2 tablespoons olive oil

2 tablespoons rock salt

6 thyme sprigs

◈ Preheat oven to 300°F (150°C/Gas Mark 2).

◈ Cut off the stem end of the tomatoes and brush each with a little olive oil. Place on a baking sheet, cut side up, and bake for 10 minutes.

◈ Sprinkle with salt and thyme sprigs. Bake for a further 5 minutes. Serve hot or warm.

asparagus
with prosciutto

serves 4

butter, for greasing

12 asparagus spears

4 thin slices prosciutto

2 tablespoons unsalted
butter, cut into small bits

ground black pepper

1/2 cup (2 oz/60 g) freshly
grated Parmesan cheese

1/2 teaspoon paprika

1 lemon, quartered

◈ Preheat an oven to 375°F (190°C/Gas Mark 4). Butter a
baking dish large enough to hold the asparagus; set aside.

◈ Gently bend each asparagus spear until it snaps; discard
end of stalk.

◈ Pour 1 inch (2 cm) water into a saucepan or frying pan
and bring to a boil. Add the asparagus and cook, uncovered,
over high heat until tender but firm, 3–4 minutes. Drain well.

◈ Divide the asparagus into 4 bundles of 3 stalks each.
Wrap 1 prosciutto slice around the center of each bundle.
Place the bundles in the prepared dish. Dot with the butter,
season to taste with pepper, and sprinkle evenly with the
cheese. Place in the oven for 5 minutes to brown the cheese.

◈ Remove from the oven, dust with the paprika, and serve
hot with the lemon quarters.

creamy
carrots and parsnips

serves 4–6 as an accompaniment

3 medium parsnips, peeled and cut into thin sticks
3 medium carrots, peeled and cut into thin sticks

CREAM SAUCE
1/3 cup (3 fl oz/90 ml) plain yogurt or sour cream
1/3 cup (3 fl oz/90 ml) mayonnaise
1/3 cup (3 fl oz/90 ml) milk
1/2 teaspoon dried basil, crushed
1/2 teaspoon dried thyme, crushed
1/4 teaspoon salt
1/8 teaspoon pepper

✧ Place parsnips and carrots in a steamer basket over boiling water in a medium saucepan. Cover and steam until vegetables are crisp-tender, 7–10 minutes.

✧ Meanwhile, for the sauce, combine the yogurt or sour cream, mayonnaise, milk, basil, thyme, salt, and pepper. Mix well.

✧ Drain vegetables; return to pan. Add sauce; cook, stirring, over low heat just until heated through (do not boil). Transfer to a warmed serving bowl and serve at once.

barley with leeks and brussels sprouts

1 cup (8 fl oz/250 ml) water

1 oz (30 g) quick-cooking barley, or
2 oz (60 g) pearl barley, or
2 oz (60 g) bulgur (burghul) wheat
or long-grain rice

10 oz (315 g) brussels sprouts,
halved lengthwise

2 tablespoons butter

1 red, yellow, or green bell pepper
(capsicum), chopped

1 leek, thinly sliced

1/2 teaspoon salt

1/2 teaspoon dried marjoram, crushed

ground black pepper

❖ In a small saucepan, bring the water to a boil. Stir in grain, return to boil, then reduce heat. Cover and simmer until tender (10–12 minutes for quick-cooking barley, 45–50 minutes for pearl barley, 12–15 minutes for bulgur, and 15 minutes for rice). Remove from heat. Let stand, covered, for 5 minutes. Drain.

❖ Cook the brussels sprouts, covered, in boiling salted water to cover for 5 minutes; drain.

❖ In a large frying pan, melt the butter. Add sprouts, bell pepper, and leek and cook, stirring, until sprouts are crisp-tender, 5–8 minutes. Stir in the cooked grain, salt, marjoram, and pepper to taste. Cook over low heat for 5 minutes more, stirring occasionally. Serve immediately.

sautéed
celery and carrots

serves 4 as an
accompaniment

2 teaspoons sesame seeds

1 tablespoon butter

3 medium carrots, peeled and
thinly bias sliced

4 ribs (stalks) celery, peeled and
thinly bias sliced

1–2 teaspoons honey

¼ teaspoon salt

✧ Toast the sesame seeds: Spread the seeds in a thin layer on an ungreased shallow baking sheet and bake in a preheated 350°F (180°C/Gas Mark 4) oven for 10–15 minutes, or until light golden brown, stirring once or twice. Transfer to a small dish and set aside.

✧ In a large frying pan, melt the butter. Add the carrot and cook over medium-high heat for 1 minute, stirring frequently. Add celery; cook for 4–5 minutes, or until vegetables are crisp-tender, stirring frequently. Stir in honey to taste, sesame seeds, and salt. Serve hot.

broccoli-noodle stir-fry

serves 6 as an
accompaniment

3 oz (90 g) dried fine noodles

SAUCE

5 fl oz (150 ml) chicken stock

2 teaspoons cornflour

1½ teaspoons soy sauce

1 teaspoon rice wine vinegar
or white vinegar

pinch of crushed dried chiles

1 tablespoon vegetable oil

2 teaspoons toasted (Asian)
sesame oil

10 oz (300 g) broccoli florets

❖ In a large saucepan, bring 2 quarts (2 l) water to a boil. Add the noodles and boil, uncovered, until just tender, 5–7 minutes. (Or, cook according to package directions.) Drain.

❖ Meanwhile, for the sauce, combine the stock, cornflour, soy sauce, vinegar, and crushed dried chiles to taste in a small bowl. Set aside.

❖ In a wok or large frying pan, heat the vegetable oil and sesame oil over medium–high heat. Add the broccoli and stir-fry until crisp-tender, 3–4 minutes. Stir the sauce and add to the wok or frying pan along with the cooked noodles. Cook, stirring, until thickened and bubbly, then continue to cook, stirring, for 1 minute more. Serve at once.

eggplant
in spicy sauce

serves 8

Eggplant (aubergine) has been eaten in China since at least 600 BC. The flavor and texture of eggplant lend themselves well to quite strong flavors, such as the spices used in this dish.

4 medium eggplants (aubergines)

3 tablespoons peanut oil

8 oz (250 g) ground (minced) pork

2 tablespoons peeled and minced fresh ginger

6 large cloves garlic, minced

2 green (spring) onions, chopped

1 teaspoon hot chile bean paste (available at Chinese food stores)

SEASONINGS

½ cup (4 fl oz/125 ml) chicken stock

3 tablespoons light soy sauce

good pinch of ground white pepper

1 teaspoon sugar

1 tablespoon cornstarch (cornflour), mixed with a little cold water

✥ Slice the eggplants in half crosswise and then into thick finger-length pieces.

✥ Bring a large pot of water to a boil. Add the eggplant and quickly return to a boil. Drain immediately and refresh in cold water. (The eggplant should still be firm, not mushy.) Transfer to a plate and set aside.

✥ Preheat a wok or large frying pan over medium–high heat. Add the peanut oil and heat until it reaches smoking point.

✥ Add the ground pork and stir-fry until it changes color. Add the ginger, garlic, and green onion and stir-fry until fragrant. Add the hot chile bean paste and mix through. Add the eggplant and toss quickly over high heat. Add all of the seasonings and cook, stirring constantly, until the sauce thickens and coats the pieces. Serve hot, with steamed rice.

garlic green beans

1 tablespoon peanut oil

*10 large cloves garlic,
peeled*

*2 cups (16 fl oz/500 ml)
chicken stock*

*1 lb (500 g) green beans,
topped and tailed*

*1 tablespoon cornstarch
(cornflour), mixed with
2 tablespoons cold water,
for thickening*

◈ In a large frying pan, combine the oil and whole garlic cloves. Stir over medium heat until the garlic is lightly golden, about 2 minutes. Add the stock, cover, and simmer until the garlic is tender when pierced, about 5 minutes.

◈ Bring the stock back to a boil and add the beans. Cook, covered, just until the beans are crisp-tender, 3–4 minutes. With tongs, lift out the beans and arrange on a serving plate.

◈ Stir the cornstarch thickening into the stock in the frying pan. Bring to a boil, stirring until thickened. Spoon the sauce and garlic over the beans. Serve hot.

broccoli rabe
with olives

serves 4

8 stalks broccoli rabe
(Italian broccoli/
rapini/broccolini)

3 tablespoons olive oil

1 tablespoon
red wine vinegar

juice of 1/2 lemon

salt and
ground black pepper

1 tablespoon
well-drained capers

1/2 cup (2 1/2 oz/75 g) pitted
black olives, chopped

❖ Trim broccoli stalks and discard the coarse leaves; pare stem to remove coarse skin if desired. Split each broccoli stalk lengthwise into thin spears (the number depends upon the thickness of the stalks).

❖ Fill a saucepan with just enough water to cover the broccoli once it is added. Bring to a boil. Add the broccoli and cook, uncovered, over high heat until tender but firm, 4–5 minutes. (If cooked quickly, broccoli will retain its bright color.) Drain and place in a serving dish.

❖ Immediately pour the olive oil over the broccoli, add the vinegar, and carefully toss. Add the lemon juice and salt and pepper to taste. Toss again. Add the capers and olives, turning the broccoli gently until thoroughly combined. Serve at room temperature.

chinese cabbage
with sesame seeds

serves 4

2 tablespoons sesame seeds

1½ cups (12 fl oz/375 ml) vegetable stock

4 green (spring) onions

1 small head Chinese (napa) cabbage, thinly sliced lengthwise and then cut in half crosswise

2 tablespoons unsalted butter

½ teaspoon crushed dried chiles

salt and ground white pepper

❖ Place the sesame seeds in a small, ungreased frying pan over medium-low heat and stir until lightly colored, 2–3 minutes. Set aside.

❖ Pour the stock into a large frying pan over high heat and boil until the stock is slightly reduced, 2–3 minutes.

❖ Cut the green onions in half lengthwise, then cut into long, thin strips. Add to the boiling stock.

❖ Add the cabbage and reduce the heat to medium. Cook, stirring occasionally, until tender, about 5 minutes. The stock should be almost totally absorbed.

❖ Stir in the butter, sesame seeds, crushed dried chiles, and salt and pepper to taste. Serve hot.

green beans
with bacon

*½ lb (250 g) small,
tender green beans
of uniform size,
trimmed if desired*

*4 slices (rashers) bacon,
cut into small dice*

*1 tablespoon
unsalted butter*

*2 green (spring) onions,
green tops only,
finely chopped*

ground black pepper

❖ Fill a frying pan with just enough water to cover the beans once they are added. Bring to a boil. Add the beans, cover, and cook over medium heat until barely tender, 6–7 minutes. Drain well and set aside.

❖ Cook the bacon in the same pan over medium heat, stirring constantly, until crisp, 2–4 minutes. Using a slotted spoon, transfer to paper towels to drain. Pour off the drippings and wipe out the pan with a paper towel.

❖ Melt the butter in the same pan over medium heat. Add the onions and sauté gently just until soft, about 1 minute. Add the beans and toss with the butter. Stir in the bacon and toss to mix well.

❖ Season to taste with pepper; serve hot or warm.

stuffed zucchini flowers
with tomato and mint

serves 4

Gentle sautéing brings out the delightful peppery flavor of fresh zucchini flowers. In this simple preparation, the tender blossoms are filled with a sheep's milk cheese, then accented with a refreshing tomato-mint sauce. Mozzarella or Fontina may be substituted for the caiotta or provolone.

16 zucchini (courgette) flowers, slightly closed

4 oz (125 g) caciotta or provolone cheese, rind removed

¼ cup (1½ oz/45 g) all-purpose (plain) flour

¼ cup (2 fl oz/60 ml) sunflower or safflower oil

TOMATO-MINT SAUCE

1 cup (8 fl oz/250 ml) purchased or homemade tomato pasta sauce

2 large fresh mint leaves, thinly sliced, or ⅛ teaspoon dried mint

◈ Trim off the long stems from the flowers and carefully spread the petals slightly apart. Cut the cheese into 16 rectangles, each ½ inch (12 mm) wide by ½ inch (12 mm) thick by 1 inch (2.5 cm) long, or long enough to fit snugly inside the flowers. Insert 1 piece of cheese into each flower and close the petals over the cheese.

◈ Spread the flour on a plate. Gently roll each flower in the flour, carefully turning to coat lightly but evenly. Transfer to a plate.

◈ In a large frying pan over medium heat, warm the oil. When hot, add the stuffed flowers in a single layer and sauté for 2–3 minutes. Using 2 forks, carefully turn over the flowers and sauté until barely golden brown on the edges and the cheese has begun to melt, 1–2 minutes longer. The flowers should remain soft.

◈ Meanwhile, make the sauce. In a small saucepan over medium heat, warm the tomato sauce to a simmer. Add the mint and simmer for 1 minute longer.

◈ Using two forks, remove the flowers from the pan, draining any excess oil. Transfer to warmed individual plates, arranging four flowers on each plate with the stem ends toward the center. Spoon the tomato-mint sauce over the stem end of each flower. Serve immediately.

new potatoes
with lemon butter

serves 4

16 small new potatoes
(1–1½ lb/500–750 g
total weight)

2 tablespoons unsalted butter

3 tablespoons olive oil

grated zest and juice of
1 lemon

1 tablespoon snipped
fresh chives

1 tablespoon chopped
fresh basil

1 tablespoon chopped
fresh parsley

salt and ground black pepper

❖ Arrange the unpeeled potatoes in a single layer in a large pan. Add water to cover, bring to a boil over high heat, then reduce heat to low, cover, and simmer until tender but still firm, 10–12 minutes. Drain well.

❖ Warm the butter and olive oil in a frying pan over low heat. Add the lemon zest, chives, basil, parsley, potatoes, and salt and pepper to taste. Heat gently, stirring to coat the potatoes with the butter mixture. Add the lemon juice, stir well, and serve immediately.

green beans with water chestnuts

½ lb (250 g) small, tender green beans of uniform size, trimmed and cut in half lengthwise

4 large, tender inner celery stalks, trimmed and thinly sliced crosswise

½ cup (3 oz/90 g) thinly sliced water chestnuts

½ cup (4 fl oz/125 ml) olive oil

3 tablespoons red wine vinegar

few drops of soy sauce

1 tablespoon heavy (double) cream

salt and ground black pepper

❖ Fill a saucepan with just enough water to cover the beans once they are added. Bring to a boil. Add the beans, cover, and cook over medium heat until barely tender, 6–7 minutes. Drain the beans.

❖ Combine the beans, celery, and water chestnuts in a serving bowl. In a small bowl, whisk together the olive oil, vinegar, soy sauce, cream, and salt and pepper to taste. Pour the dressing over the vegetables and toss well. Serve at room temperature.

quick and easy salads

crab salad
with mango

10 oz (300 g) freshly cooked
crab meat, picked over for
shell fragments

2 tablespoons mayonnaise

2/3 cup (4 oz/125 g) peeled and
finely diced mango

1/3 cup (2 oz/60 g) roasted,
peeled, and diced
red bell pepper (capsicum)

1/4 teaspoon cayenne pepper

2 tablespoons chopped
fresh chives

salt and ground black pepper

2 cups (2 oz/60 g) mesclun or
other bitter greens

◈ Wrap the crab meat tightly in a clean kitchen towel to absorb any excess water. Place the crab meat in a bowl and add the mayonnaise. Using a fork, mix together thoroughly.

◈ Add the mango, bell pepper, cayenne pepper, half of the chives, and salt and pepper to taste. Mix gently until all the ingredients are evenly distributed.

◈ Scatter the salad greens evenly over individual plates. Divide the crab mixture equally among the plates, mounding it on top of the greens. Sprinkle the remaining chives evenly over the top and serve at once.

bean, rice, and tuna salad

serves 4–6; dressing makes
1½ cups (12 fl oz/375 ml)

Serve this satisfying salad
with bread for a complete
meal that is perfect at the
end of a hot summer's day.

3 tablespoons olive oil

1 clove garlic, crushed

¼ cup (2 fl oz/60 ml) lemon juice

1 tablespoon wine vinegar

½ green bell pepper (capsicum), chopped

1 red (Spanish) onion, chopped

½ cup (2 oz/60 g) pitted and chopped Kalamata olives

¼ teaspoon ground black pepper

7 oz (220 g) canned tuna, drained

1 lb (500 g) canned white cannellini beans, drained

3 cups (9 oz/280 g) cooked white rice

For the dressing, combine the oil, garlic, lemon juice, vinegar, bell pepper, onion, olives, and pepper in a mixing bowl. If not for immediate use, transfer to a sterilized jar and keep in the refrigerator for up to 3 days.

Place the tuna, beans, and rice in a large bowl. Pour the dressing over the top of this mixture and mix well.

Chill for several hours before serving.

recipe variation

For variety, in place of green bell pepper (capsicum), you can use yellow, orange, or red bell peppers. And instead of the red onion, try finely chopped golden (French) or purple (Asian) shallots.

avocado and
tomatillo
salad

serves 4–6

This home-style salad
showcases the wonderful
contrasts that are provided
by combining rich, creamy
avocado, sharp-tasting
tomatillos, and crunchy
croutons. The vegetables
must be at their peak of
ripeness for the best results.
The avocado should be only
slightly soft, so it will not
fall apart during tossing.

½ cup (4 fl oz/125 ml) olive oil

⅓ loaf crusty French, Italian, or sourdough bread, cut into ¾-inch (2-cm) cubes

salt to taste, plus 1 teaspoon

ground pepper to taste, plus ½ teaspoon

2 ripe avocados, pitted, peeled, and cut into ¾-inch (2-cm) cubes

2 cups (12 oz/375 g) red and/or yellow cherry tomatoes, halved

2 bunches cilantro (fresh coriander), about 6 oz (185 g) total weight, stemmed

5 tomatillos, husked and quartered

1 tablespoon fresh lime juice

2 tablespoons distilled white or white wine vinegar

lettuce leaves

6 green (spring) onions, thinly sliced

✤ In a frying pan over medium heat, warm ¼ cup (2 fl oz/60 ml) of the olive oil. Add the bread cubes and shake the pan to coat the cubes lightly on all sides. Sprinkle with salt and pepper to taste, reduce the heat to medium-low, and toast, shaking the pan occasionally, until golden brown on all sides, about 15 minutes. Remove from the heat and let cool.

✤ In a bowl, combine the avocado, cherry tomatoes, and cilantro; set aside. In a blender or a food processor fitted with the metal blade, combine the tomatillos, lime juice, vinegar, the remaining ¼ cup (2 fl oz/60 ml) olive oil, the 1 teaspoon salt, and the ½ teaspoon pepper. Blend well to form a smooth dressing.

✤ Pour the dressing over the avocado mixture and toss lightly to mix. When almost fully mixed, add the croutons and continue to toss until all ingredients are evenly distributed.

✤ To serve, line a platter or individual salad bowls with lettuce leaves and spoon the avocado mixture on top. Garnish with the green onions and serve immediately.

summer squash and rice salad

serves 4–6

The mixture of rice and vegetables in this salad provides a balanced flavor and a texture that doesn't become soggy. Success depends upon cooking and seasoning all the components separately, so that the flavors remain pronounced when the ingredients are combined. This recipe is also good for using up leftovers.

½ cup (4 fl oz/125 ml) olive oil

5 assorted small summer squashes, such as zucchini (courgettes), yellow crookneck or straightneck, or pattypan, in any combination, trimmed and cut into ¼-inch (6-mm) dice

salt and ground black pepper

1 yellow onion, diced

2 cloves garlic, crushed

2 teaspoons ground cumin

2 tablespoons distilled white or cider vinegar

2 cups (10 oz/300 g) cooked rice, at room temperature

½ cup (¾ oz/20 g) coarsely chopped fresh parsley

shredded lettuce leaves

In a frying pan over high heat, warm 2 tablespoons of the olive oil. Add one-third of the squash and season to taste with salt and pepper. Sauté, stirring often, until lightly browned and slightly soft, 1–2 minutes. Transfer to a bowl. Cook the remaining squash, in 2 batches, in the same way, using 2 tablespoons oil with each batch. Let the mixture cool.

In the same frying pan, heat the remaining 2 tablespoons oil over medium heat. Add the onion and sauté until lightly golden, 3–5 minutes. Stir in the garlic and cook for a few seconds. Add the cumin, reduce the heat to low, and sauté for about 2 minutes longer. Add to the bowl holding the squashes.

Add the vinegar, rice, and parsley and toss to mix well.

Taste and adjust the seasonings. (At this point, the salad can be covered and refrigerated for up to 3 days. Bring to room temperature before serving.)

To serve, line individual plates with lettuce and spoon the salad on top. Serve at once.

salad dressings

green dressing

½ cup (1 oz/30 g) chopped fresh parsley

3 green (spring) onions, chopped

¾ teaspoon dried oregano

1 tablespoon anchovy paste

½ cup (4 oz/125 g) low-fat cottage cheese

⅓ cup (3 fl oz/90 ml) non-fat yogurt

2 tablespoons mayonnaise

2 cloves garlic, minced

2 ripe avocados, peeled and pitted

2 tablespoons lemon juice

❖ Combine all of the ingredients in a food processor and process until smooth. The mixture will be fairly thin.

❖ Spoon into a sterilized jar. Seal or cover the jar and refrigerate for 1 hour to thicken, or chill in the refrigerator for up to 2 days.

makes 2 cups (16 fl oz/500 ml)

tomato dressing

1 medium tomato, seeded, drained, and finely chopped

½ cup (4 fl oz/125 ml) olive oil

2 tablespoons cider vinegar

2 teaspoons honey

1 clove garlic, minced

1 teaspoon soy sauce

¼ teaspoon paprika

salt

small dash hot-pepper sauce such as Tabasco

❖ Combine all of the ingredients in a sterilized jar with a tight-fitting lid.

❖ Cover, shake well, and chill until required. This recipe will keep in the refrigerator for about 1 week.

makes ¾ cup (6 fl oz/185 ml)

classic dressing

4 small green (spring) onions

½ cup (½ oz/15 g) fresh parsley

1½ teaspoons fresh tarragon

1 tablespoon anchovy paste

½ cup (4 oz/125 g) low-fat cottage cheese

¼ cup (2 fl oz/60 ml) non-fat yogurt

2 tablespoons mayonnaise

2 tablespoons lemon juice

◈ Chop the green onions, including 7.5 cm (3 inches) of the top green parts. In a food processor or blender, combine the green onions, parsley, tarragon, anchovy paste, cottage cheese, yogurt, mayonnaise, and lemon juice.

◈ Process until the mixture is completely puréed. The dressing will be thin. Pour into a sterilized jar, cover, and refrigerate for at least 30 minutes before using. The dressing will keep in the refrigerator for up to 2 days.

makes 1 cup (8 fl oz/250 ml)

shallot dressing

⅔ cup (6 fl oz/185 ml) water

1 teaspoon arrowroot

1 tablespoon Dijon mustard

⅓ cup (1¾ oz/50 g) finely chopped golden (French) shallots

¼ cup (2 fl oz/60 ml) sherry vinegar

◈ Combine the water and arrowroot in a saucepan. Bring to a gentle boil, stirring constantly. Remove from heat when a gravy-like consistency is reached, 1–2 minutes.

◈ Place the saucepan into a mixing bowl that is one-fourth filled with ice cubes and water. Allow contents of saucepan to reach room temperature. Mix the remaining ingredients into the arrowroot mixture.

◈ Pour into a sterilized jar, cover, label if desired, and chill well before using. This dressing will keep for 3–4 days in the refrigerator.

makes 1½ cups (12 fl oz/375 ml)

greek salad

DRESSING

½ cup (4 fl oz/125 ml) extra-virgin olive oil

2–3 tablespoons fresh lemon juice

3 tablespoons dried oregano

cracked black pepper

1 clove garlic, finely minced (optional)

2–3 cups (2–3 oz/60–90 g) torn assorted salad greens
such as romaine (cos), escarole (endive), or frisée

4 small ripe tomatoes, cored and cut into wedges

1 large cucumber, peeled, seeded, and cut into wedges

1 red (Spanish) onion, thinly sliced into rings

2 small green bell peppers (capsicums), seeded,
deribbed, and thinly sliced crosswise into rings

½ lb (250 g) feta cheese, coarsely crumbled

20 Kalamata olives

❖ To make the dressing, in a bowl, stir together the olive oil, lemon juice, oregano, cracked pepper to taste, and the garlic, if using. Set aside.

❖ In a large salad bowl, combine the greens, tomatoes, cucumber, onion, and bell peppers. Drizzle the dressing over the top and toss gently to mix. Sprinkle the feta cheese and olives over the top and serve at once.

tomato, mozzarella, and basil salad

serves 4–6

*¾ lb (375 g) fresh
mozzarella cheese, drained*

*4 tablespoons (2 fl oz/60 ml)
extra-virgin olive oil*

salt and pepper

*12 fresh basil leaves,
thinly sliced*

*2 tablespoons coarsely chopped
fresh flat-leaf (Italian) parsley*

*2 pints (12 oz/375 g) round
and/or pear-shaped cherry
tomatoes, in a mixture of colors*

*¼ cup (1½ oz/45 g) Moroccan
olives or other oil-cured olives*

❖ If using large balls of mozzarella, cut them into
½-inch (12-mm) dice. If using smaller balls, cut them
into quarters. In a bowl, toss the mozzarella with half
of the olive oil and salt and pepper to taste. Add half
of the basil and half of the parsley. Toss gently.

❖ If using round cherry tomatoes, cut them in half.
If using pear-shaped tomatoes, leave them whole. In
another bowl, combine the tomatoes with the remaining
olive oil, salt and pepper to taste, and the remaining
basil and parsley. Toss gently.

❖ Mound the mozzarella in the center of individual
plates. Make a ring of the seasoned tomatoes around
the edge and garnish with the olives. Serve immediately.

tricolor coleslaw

serves 6–8

DRESSING

3 tablespoons cider vinegar

1 tablespoon sugar

2 cups (16 fl oz/500 ml) mayonnaise

¼ teaspoon salt

¼ teaspoon ground black pepper

3 tablespoons finely chopped fresh parsley

SALAD

½ small head red cabbage, shredded
(about 3 cups/9 oz/280 g)

1 small head green cabbage, shredded
(about 5 cups/15 oz/470 g)

2 carrots, peeled and shredded
(about 1 cup/5 oz/155 g)

◈ To make the dressing, in a large serving bowl, stir together the vinegar, sugar, mayonnaise, salt, pepper, and parsley until well blended.

◈ Add the red and green cabbage and the carrot to the dressing. Using tongs, toss to coat all the vegetables evenly with the dressing.

◈ Cover with plastic wrap and chill for at least 2 hours and up to 8 hours before serving.

potato salad
with onions

8 potatoes, peeled and cubed

¼ cup (2 fl oz/60 ml)
red wine vinegar

2 tablespoons chopped dill

2 small red (Spanish)
onions, sliced

⅓ cup (3 fl oz/90 ml)
sour cream

⅓ cup (3 fl oz/90 ml)
mayonnaise

salt and ground black pepper

❖ Place the potatoes in a large saucepan. Cover with water, set over low heat, bring to a boil, and cook potatoes until tender. Drain. Add the vinegar, dill, and onions and toss gently. Cool.

❖ Combine the sour cream and mayonnaise and season with salt and plenty of ground black pepper. Gently fold into the potatoes and serve immediately.

chickpea salad
with herb vinaigrette

serves 4–6 as an accompaniment

1 cup (6 oz/185 g) dried chickpeas
(garbanzo beans)

2 medium tomatoes, skinned

3½ oz (100 g) black olives, pitted and sliced

1 red (Spanish) onion, sliced into fine rings

FRESH HERB VINAIGRETTE

5 tablespoons olive oil

2 tablespoons red wine vinegar

1 tablespoon fresh lemon juice

1 clove garlic, crushed

1 tablespoon each finely chopped fresh flat-leaf
(Italian) parsley, thyme, and rosemary

½ teaspoon sugar

salt and ground black pepper

❖ Soak the chickpeas in cold water overnight. Drain, then cook in plenty of boiling salted water until tender, about 1 hour. Drain and refresh under cold water.

❖ Halve the tomatoes, remove the seeds, and chop finely. Combine the chickpeas, tomato, olives, and onion.

❖ Combine all of the vinaigrette ingredients in a small bowl and whisk until thoroughly combined. Pour the dressing over the salad and mix until the ingredients are combined and well coated with the dressing.

❖ Serve at room temperature.

smoked trout salad

salad

serves 6

DILL DRESSING

¾ cup (6 fl oz/185 ml) olive oil

1 teaspoon dried dill

3 tablespoons champagne vinegar

salt and pepper to taste

SALAD

12 small potatoes, boiled until tender and kept warm

1 small red (Spanish) onion, diced

1 lb (500 g) smoked trout, boned, skinned, and cut into pieces

2 bunches watercress, washed and dried

◈ Warm the oil in a saucepan and, crushing the dill between your fingertips, add it to the warm oil. Add the vinegar, salt, and pepper and whisk together. (If the dressing is not being used immediately, it can be transferred to a storage container and refrigerated for up to 1 week. Bring to room temperature before combining with the warm potato mixture.)

◈ Combine the potatoes, onion, trout, and watercress in a large serving bowl.

◈ Pour the dressing over the salad. Stir to mix, breaking up the warm potatoes so that they absorb all of the dressing.

◈ Serve the salad immediately.

warm thai chicken salad

serves 6 as an appetizer or light lunch

CHICKEN AND MARINADE

4 boneless, skinless chicken breast halves
(about 1¼ lb/600 g)

3 tablespoons toasted (Asian) sesame oil

¼ cup (2 fl oz/60 ml) fresh lemon juice

¼ teaspoon salt

2 cloves garlic, crushed

1 tablespoon brown sugar

2 tablespoons finely chopped cilantro
(fresh coriander)

DRESSING

1 small red chile (seeds included if desired),
finely chopped

1 clove garlic, finely chopped

3 tablespoons extra-virgin olive oil

1 tablespoon balsamic vinegar

juice of 2 limes

1 teaspoon sweet chile sauce

SALAD

1 bunch (14 oz/440 g) mizuna, arugula
(rocket), or other salad leaves

1 red bell pepper (capsicum),
seeds removed and cut into julienne

1 cucumber, cut into julienne

2 carrots, cut into julienne

6 green (spring) onions, sliced

1 cup (1 oz/30 g) loosely packed cilantro
(fresh coriander) sprigs

1 cup (1 oz/30 g) shredded purple basil

3 tablespoons sesame seeds, toasted

◈ Place the chicken breasts between 2 sheets of plastic wrap and, using the flat side of a meat mallet, lightly pound to flatten the meat slightly. Cut each lengthwise into 4 strips. Combine all of the marinade ingredients in a shallow nonmetallic bowl and mix well. Add the chicken and toss to coat. Cover with plastic wrap and set aside in the refrigerator overnight, or at room temperature for several hours.

◈ For the dressing, combine all of the dressing ingredients in a small bowl and whisk well.

◈ Divide the salad leaves, bell pepper, cucumber, carrot, green onions, cilantro, and basil evenly among 6 individual serving plates, arranging them attractively.

◈ Heat the sesame oil in a wok or frying pan until smoking. Stir-fry the chicken until cooked through, about 3 minutes. Divide the chicken among the serving plates. Drizzle on the dressing and sprinkle with the toasted sesame seeds.

◈ Serve immediately, while the chicken is still warm.

rare roast beef salad

serves 6

DRESSING

⅓ cup (3½ fl oz/100 ml) olive oil

¼ cup (2 fl oz/60 ml) lemon juice

2 tablespoons finely chopped chives

1 tablespoon drained tiny capers

1 tablespoon finely chopped
sun-dried bell pepper (capsicum)

salt and freshly ground black pepper

MUSTARD MAYONNAISE

¼ cup (2 fl oz/60 ml) mayonnaise

1 tablespoon Dijon mustard

2 teaspoons Worcestershire sauce

dash of hot-pepper sauce, such as Tabasco

SALAD

12 large slices rare roast beef

6 oz (185 g) cherry tomatoes, halved

1 head (3½ oz/100 g) radicchio,
washed and torn

1 bunch (3½ oz/100 g) corn salad (lamb's
lettuce/mâche), washed and torn

8 oz (250 g) home-cooked or canned
artichoke hearts, halved

⅓ cup (2½ oz/75 g) tiny cornichons
(tiny gherkins or dill pickles)

❖ For the dressing, combine all of the dressing ingredients in a small bowl. Whisk until well blended.

❖ For the mustard mayonnaise, combine all of the mayonnaise ingredients in a small bowl and stir well.

❖ Divide the remaining ingredients among 6 serving plates. Spoon the dressing over and place a tablespoon of mayonnaise in the center of each salad.

food fact

Corn salad (also known as lamb's lettuce or mâche) is not a lettuce at all, but a member of the valerian family native to Britain, most of Europe, the Middle East, and North Africa. Although it can be expensive to buy, corn salad is easy to grow. In mild areas, it can be grown as a winter vegetable. The leaves are best eaten when small; if left to get large, they may become tough. Some cultivars remain sweet even when in flower.

smoked ham and camembert salad

DRESSING

½ cup (2½ oz/75 g) shelled pecans

juice of 2 lemons

1 clove garlic

¼ teaspoon salt

½ cup (4 fl oz/125 ml) olive oil

½ cup (4 fl oz/125 ml) sour cream

2 tablespoons finely chopped chives

grated zest of 1 lemon

SALAD

1 head butter (Boston) lettuce, washed and torn

1½ oz (45 g) snow pea sprouts

2 Granny Smith apples, cut into julienne and sprinkled with the juice of ½ lemon

6½ oz (200 g) smoked ham, cut into julienne

6½ oz (200 g) camembert, at room temperature, thinly sliced

2½ oz (75 g) pecan nuts, toasted and roughly chopped

For the dressing, chop the pecans finely in a food processor fitted with the metal blade. Add the lemon juice, garlic, salt, and oil and process until thoroughly combined. Add the sour cream, chives, and lemon zest and combine thoroughly.

Arrange the salad ingredients on a serving platter or individual plates. Spoon the dressing over the salad. Serve immediately.

recipe hint

Instead of the ham, you could use an equal weight of finely shredded leftover chicken, turkey, or roast beef, or purchased smoked chicken cut into julienne.

quick and easy
desserts

banana fritters

6 small semi-ripe bananas

BATTER

½ cup (2½ oz/75 g) all-purpose (plain) flour

2 tablespoons cornstarch (cornflour)

¼ cup (2 oz/60 g) sugar

¼ teaspoon salt

½ cup (4 fl oz/125 ml) water

vegetable oil, for deep-frying

confectioners' (icing) sugar

ground cinnamon

❖ Peel bananas; cut crosswise into 3-inch (7.5-cm) lengths.

❖ For the batter, in a bowl, sift together the flour, cornstarch, sugar, and salt. Gradually add the water, stirring constantly, until the batter is smooth and thick enough to lightly coat the back of a spoon.

❖ Preheat a deep saucepan over medium-high heat. Pour in oil to a depth of 1½ inches (4 cm) and heat to 375°F (190°C) on a deep-frying thermometer. Add the bananas to the batter. Using tongs, lift out the banana pieces one at a time, allowing excess batter to drip into the bowl, and carefully lower into the hot oil. Do not crowd the pan; the fruit must float freely. Deep-fry, turning often, until golden brown, about 2 minutes.

❖ Transfer to paper towels to drain. Repeat with the remaining banana pieces.

❖ Arrange the bananas on a warmed platter and dust with confectioners' sugar and cinnamon. Serve hot.

poached autumn pears with mascarpone and ginger

serves 4

In Italy, pears are often poached with sugar in a dry white or red wine. This recipe cooks them instead in a naturally sweet dessert wine. A good choice is Moscato d'Asti from Piedmont, which produces a delicious, honeylike syrup when reduced. If it is not available, any light, fruity dessert wine may be used.

POACHED PEARS

2 large ripe pears

1 1/2 cups (12 fl oz/375 ml) Moscato d'Asti wine (see note)

1 stick cinnamon, 3 inches (7.5 cm) long, broken in half

1/2 teaspoon allspice berries or 1 whole clove

TOPPING

1/2 cup (3 oz/90 g) mascarpone cheese

2 teaspoons confectioners' (icing) sugar, or to taste

1 teaspoon milk

2 teaspoons chopped candied (glacé) ginger

4 fresh mint sprigs (optional)

⬥ To poach the pears, cut the pears in half lengthwise, then core and peel the halves. In a saucepan, combine the wine, cinnamon, and allspice berries or the clove and bring to a boil. Place the pears in the liquid, cored side down, reduce the heat to medium–low, and simmer for 4–5 minutes. Turn the pears over and poach until barely soft when pierced with a sharp knife, 4–5 minutes longer.

⬥ Using a slotted spoon, carefully place each pear half, cored side down, in the center of an individual plate.

⬥ Reduce the poaching liquid over medium heat until it forms a thick syrup, about 5 minutes. Strain through a fine-mesh sieve into a clean container. Discard the contents of the sieve.

⬥ For the topping, in a small bowl, whisk together the mascarpone, sugar, and milk until smooth.

⬥ To serve, cut each pear half into a fan shape: Hold a paring knife at a 45-degree angle to the pear, and make slashes completely through it, but leave the top intact. Gently press on the slices to spread them out, and then drizzle the reduced syrup over the top. Put a dollop of the mascarpone mixture at the top of each pear. Sprinkle evenly with the candied ginger and garnish with the mint sprigs, if desired.

vanilla ice cream with strawberries and balsamic vinegar

serves 4

1 pt (500 ml) vanilla
ice cream

2½ cups (10 oz/315 g)
strawberries,
stems removed,
halved lengthwise

¼ cup (2 fl oz/60 ml)
balsamic vinegar,
or to taste

1 tablespoon sugar

coarsely ground black
pepper

❖ Remove the ice cream from the freezer and let stand at room temperature until it is soft enough to stir into the strawberries, 10–15 minutes, depending upon on how cold the freezer is.

❖ Meanwhile, in a bowl large enough to accommodate the ice cream eventually, stir together the strawberries, ¼ cup (2 fl oz/60 ml) balsamic vinegar, sugar, and pepper to taste. The vinegar and sugar will mix with the berries' natural juices to create a saucelike consistency. Taste and add more vinegar if needed.

❖ When the ice cream is soft enough, add it to the berry mixture. Immediately stir together until the berries and ice cream are evenly distributed. Spoon into tall wineglasses and serve at once.

summer berry
pudding

serves 8

1 loaf day-old white bread,
crusts removed (about 15 slices)

1½ cups (12 oz/375 g)
raspberries

1 cup (8 oz/250 g) red currants

1½ cups (12 oz/375 g)
blackberries

1½ cups (12 oz/375 g)
blueberries

¾ cup (6 oz/185 g)
superfine (caster) sugar

¾ cup (6 oz/185 g)
strawberries, sliced

heavy (double) cream, to serve

extra berries, to serve (optional)

❖ Line a medium-size bowl or pudding basin with the bread, reserving enough to make a lid.

❖ Combine the raspberries, red currants, blackberries, blueberries, and sugar in a medium saucepan. Cook over moderate heat until the juice starts to run, about 8 minutes. Remove from heat and add strawberries. Pour into the bread-lined bowl and cover the top with the reserved pieces of bread.

❖ Lay a piece of plastic wrap over the top and place a plate over this. Weight down the plate with two cans or a heavy weight.

❖ Refrigerate for at least 24 hours. Turn out onto a plate and serve with heavy (double) cream and extra berries, if desired.

serves 12

13 oz (410 g) bittersweet
chocolate, coarsely chopped

½ cup (4 oz/125 g)
butter, at room temperature

4 egg yolks

2½ oz (75 g) confectioners'
(icing) sugar

½ teaspoon ground
cinnamon

2 cups (16 fl oz/500 ml) cold
heavy (double) cream

2–3 drops vanilla extract
(essence)

RASPBERRY SAUCE

1 cup (4 oz/125 g) raspberries

3–4 tablespoons
confectioners' (icing) sugar,
or to taste, sifted

1 tablespoon orange juice,
Cointreau, or liqueur
of your choice

❖ For the chocolate terrine, melt the chocolate in the top of a double boiler or in a microwave oven. Add the butter and stir until smooth.

❖ In large bowl, using an electric mixer on medium to high speed, beat the egg yolks with the confectioners' sugar and cinnamon until foamy. Beat in the chocolate mixture; set aside to cool.

❖ Whip the cream, add the vanilla extract, and continue to whip until the cream forms peaks. Fold it into the chocolate batter.

❖ Line an 11-inch (28-cm) cake mold with waxed (greaseproof) paper and pour in the batter. Cover and refrigerate for 12–24 hours.

❖ To make the sauce, in a food processor fitted with the metal blade, purée the raspberries. Pass through a fine-mesh sieve into a bowl; discard the contents of the sieve. Stir in the sugar and the orange juice or liqueur. Chill before serving.

❖ To serve, unmold the cake and serve it sliced, with the sauce.

chocolate terrine
with raspberry sauce

peaches and berries
in toffee syrup

serves 8

8 ripe but firm peaches

3 cups (24 fl oz/750 ml) water

2 cups (16 oz/500 g) sugar

2 cups (8 oz/250 g) raspberries

2 cups (8 oz/250 g) blackberries

❖ Place the peaches in a bowl of boiling water for a few minutes or until softened. Remove from water and, when cool enough to handle, peel.

❖ Place the sugar and 2 cups (16 fl oz/ 500 ml) of the water in a saucepan. Stir over low heat, without boiling, until the sugar dissolves. Bring to a boil, without stirring, and boil rapidly until the syrup turns a pale golden-brown, forming toffee. Remove from the heat. Add the remaining 1 cup (8 fl oz/250 ml) water (take care, as the mixture will spatter), then stir over medium heat until toffee melts; remove from heat.

❖ Place the peaches in a bowl and pour the syrup over. Allow to cool. When ready to serve, arrange peaches and berries in a bowl and spoon syrup over.

mocha zabaglione

serves 6

8 egg yolks

½ cup (4 oz/125 g) sugar

2 tablespoons unsweetened cocoa powder, plus extra for dusting

¼ cup (2 fl oz/60 ml) marsala

¼ cup (2 fl oz/60 ml) coffee liqueur

½ cup (4 fl oz/125 ml) sweet white wine

fresh fruit or sponge finger cookies (savoiardi/ladyfingers), to serve (optional)

❖ Place the egg yolks, sugar, and cocoa in the top of a double boiler or in a heatproof bowl and, using an electric mixer on medium to high speed, beat until combined. Place the pan or bowl over a saucepan of simmering water. Add the Marsala and coffee liqueur and beat until combined and creamy. Add the wine and continue to beat for about 10 minutes, or until thick and creamy. Remove from the heat and stir vigorously with a wooden spoon. Pour into glasses and dust top with additional cocoa. Serve immediately.

❖ This dessert can be served with fresh fruit or sponge finger cookies, if desired.

creamy
lime pie

*¾ cup (6 fl oz/180 ml)
fresh lime juice*

*1 lb (500 g) cream cheese,
at room temperature*

*1 can (14 fl oz/440 ml)
sweetened condensed milk*

finely grated zest of 1 lime

*1 purchased or homemade pastry shell
(9–10 inches/23–25 cm),
cooked and cooled*

1 cup (8 fl oz/250 ml) crème fraîche

*¼ cup (1 oz/30 g) confectioners'
(icing) sugar*

1 lime, for garnish

❖ In a food processor fitted with the metal blade, combine the lime juice, cream cheese, and condensed milk. Process until smooth, pausing the machine often to scrape down the sides of the work bowl. Add the lime zest and process to mix thoroughly. Pour into the pie shell and place in the refrigerator.

❖ In a bowl, using a whisk, beat the crème fraîche and confectioners' sugar until soft peaks form. Using a rubber spatula, spread the mixture over the top of the pie, creating peaks evenly over the surface. Slice 8 thin slices from the center of the lime and cut each slice once from the center to the edge. Form a twist from each slice and place these twists, evenly spaced, on the pie.

❖ Cover and chill for 4–6 hours or as long as overnight before serving.

english trifle

serves 6–8

SHERRY CUSTARD

3 cups (24 fl oz/750 ml) purchased or homemade custard

3 tablespoons cream sherry

TRIFLE

1 medium-sized vanilla or lemon sponge cake or other plain cake

2 cups (16 fl oz/500 ml) heavy (double) cream

¼ cup (1 oz/30 g) confectioners' (icing) sugar

1 cup (4 oz/125 g) raspberries

1½ cups (6 oz/185 g) strawberries, hulled and sliced

1 cup (10 oz/310 g) strawberry jam

¾ cup (6 fl oz/180 ml) cream sherry

1 cup (3½ oz) blanched sliced (flaked) almonds, toasted

english trifle

❖ To make the sherry custard, combine the custard and the 3 tablespoons cream sherry. Whisk until thoroughly blended.

❖ To make the trifle, cut the cooled cake into slices ¼ inch (5 mm) thick; set aside.

❖ In a bowl, combine the cream and confectioners' sugar. Using an electric mixer on medium to high speed, beat until soft peaks form. Cover and refrigerate.

❖ To assemble the trifle, pour about ½ cup (4 fl oz/125 ml) of the custard mixture into the bottom of a 3-qt (3-l) glass bowl. Scatter one-fourth of the raspberries and strawberries over the custard. Spread one side of the cake slices with the jam. Arrange enough of the cake slices, jam-side up, in a single layer to cover the custard, then sprinkle about 3 tablespoons of the sherry over the top. Sprinkle some of the toasted almond slices over the cake. Top with a layer of the whipped cream, spreading the cream to the edges. Starting with the custard, repeat the layers in the same manner until all the ingredients are used up, ending with a layer of whipped cream.

❖ Garnish with the remaining ½ cup (2 oz/60 g) strawberries. Cover and refrigerate for at least 2 hours before serving.

strawberry tortoni

*3 cups (24 fl oz/750 ml)
heavy (double) cream*

*1⅓ cups (12 oz/375 g)
strawberries, roughly chopped*

*¾ cup (3 oz/90 g)
slivered almonds, toasted*

9 amaretti cookies, crushed

⅓ cup (3 fl oz/90 ml) brandy

3 egg whites

*¾ cup (6 oz/185 g)
superfine (caster) sugar*

½ teaspoon baking powder

◈ Whip the cream and set aside. Mix the strawberries, almonds, crushed amaretti, and brandy in a bowl. Set aside for 10 minutes.

◈ With an electric mixer on medium to high speed, beat the egg whites until they are stiff and soft peaks form. Slowly add the sugar and baking powder, and beat until shiny.

◈ Fold the beaten egg whites and the strawberry mixture into the cream, combining the mixtures lightly but thoroughly. Pour into the desired mold or individual serving dishes and freeze, covered, for 4–5 hours, depending on the size of the dish. Serve frozen.

peaches
poached in wine

One of the wonders of summer, peaches are showcased in this easy dessert. The amount of sugar added to the poaching liquid will depend upon the wine's relative dryness; the liquid should be just sweet enough to heighten the natural sweetness of the peaches. To dress up the dish, top each serving with a dollop of mascarpone.

6 yellow- or white-fleshed peaches

1 bottle (24 fl oz/750 ml) fruity white or red still or sparkling wine, or Champagne

⅓–⅔ cup (3–5 oz/90–155 g) sugar

1 vanilla bean, split lengthwise

mascarpone cheese, to serve (optional)

✧ Bring a saucepan three-fourths full of water to a boil. One at a time, dip the peaches into the boiling water for 5 seconds. Lift out with a slotted spoon and, using a sharp paring knife, peel the peaches. Halve each fruit along the natural line and remove the pits.

✧ In a saucepan large enough to hold all the peaches in a single layer, combine the wine, ⅓ cup (3 oz/90 g) of the sugar, and the vanilla bean. Place over low heat and stir until the sugar dissolves. Taste and add more sugar as needed to achieve a pleasant sweetness (see note). Bring to a simmer, add the peaches, and simmer until barely tender, 2–5 minutes, depending upon their ripeness.

✧ Transfer the peaches and their cooking liquid to a deep glass bowl (the peaches should be completely covered by the liquid) and let cool to room temperature. Cover tightly with plastic wrap and refrigerate for at least 2 days or for up to 3 days.

✧ To serve, using a slotted spoon, transfer the peach halves to large wineglasses, placing 2 halves in each glass. Half-fill each glass with the poaching liquid and serve.

mixed berry shortcake

Adding other summer berries to this recipe makes it even more delightful. You can also substitute an equal quantity of peaches, apricots, or plums. If you like, replace the whipped cream with a drizzle of heavy (double) cream, a more traditional embellishment.

2 cups (8 oz/250 g) strawberries, hulled and thickly sliced

2 cups (8 oz/250 g) raspberries

2 cups (8 oz/250 g) blackberries

2–3 tablespoons confectioners' (icing) sugar

2 teaspoons Grand Marnier or other orange liqueur

SHORTCAKE

2 cups (10 oz/315 g) all-purpose (plain) flour

1 tablespoon baking powder

½ teaspoon salt

2 tablespoons granulated sugar

⅓ cup (3 oz/90 g) unsalted butter, chilled, cut into ½-inch (12-mm) pieces

1 cup (8 fl oz/250 ml) heavy (double) cream

1 cup (8 fl oz/250 ml) heavy (double) cream, extra, whipped to soft peaks and chilled

◈ In a large bowl, combine all the berries, the confectioners' sugar, and Grand Marnier. Toss to mix. Set aside. Preheat an oven to 425°F (220°C/Gas Mark 6).

◈ The shortcake may be made in a food processor or by hand. For the food processor method, combine the flour, baking powder, salt, and granulated sugar in the bowl of a food processor fitted with the metal blade. Process briefly to mix. Add the butter and, using on-off pulses, process until the mixture resembles coarse crumbs. With the motor running, slowly add the 1 cup (8 fl oz/250 ml) unwhipped cream, processing until the mixture forms a soft dough.

◈ To make the shortcake by hand, in a large bowl, combine the flour, baking powder, salt, and granulated sugar. Using a pastry blender, 2 knives, or your fingertips, cut or rub in the butter until the mixture resembles coarse crumbs. Using a fork, gradually mix in the 1 cup (8 fl oz/250 ml) unwhipped cream until the dough holds together.

◈ Turn out the dough made by either method onto a lightly floured board and knead briefly. Roll out the dough into a 6- x -12-inch (15- x 30-cm) rectangle ½ inch (12 mm) thick. Cut into eight 3-inch (7.5-cm) squares. Place the squares at least 3 inches (7.5 cm) apart on an ungreased baking sheet. Bake until the tops are light brown, 10–12 minutes.

◈ To assemble, split the shortcakes in half horizontally and place the bottoms, cut side up, on 8 individual dessert plates. Spoon an equal amount of the berries over each shortcake bottom, then spoon an equal amount of the whipped cream over the berries. Place the shortcake top gently over the cream and berries and serve immediately.

sweet sauces

orange ginger dip

This is wonderful when used as a dip for fresh fruit, especially strawberries, or served with peaches and vanilla ice cream or mascarpone.

1 cup (8 oz/250 g) cream cheese, softened

1 tablespoon sugar

1 tablespoon orange zest

2 teaspoons finely chopped fresh ginger

1 teaspoon ground ginger

6–8 tablespoons fresh orange juice

pinch salt

❖ Combine all of the ingredients in a bowl. Stir the mixture until smooth.

❖ Cover and refrigerate until required. This dip will keep for 3–4 days.

makes 1½ cups (12 fl oz/375 ml)

chocolate sauce

Serve cold with ice cream, or warm with a chocolate fudge cake or brownies.

1 cup (8 fl oz/250 ml) heavy (double) cream

1 tablespoon unsalted butter

4 oz (125 g) semisweet cooking chocolate, chopped

1 tablespoon dark rum, brandy, or liqueur of your choice

❖ Bring cream and butter to a boil in a small saucepan. Add chocolate and rum, remove from heat, and stir until chocolate is melted.

❖ The sauce will keep, refrigerated, for up to 3 days, but is best eaten immediately.

makes 1½ cups (12 fl oz/375 ml)

lemon sauce

Serve with fresh sponge cake filled with jam and cream.

3 eggs

1 cup (8 oz/250 g) sugar

2 teaspoons finely grated lemon zest

½ cup (4 fl oz/125 ml) fresh lemon juice

1 cup (8 fl oz/250 ml) water

pinch salt

❖ Beat eggs in a large bowl until foamy; add the sugar in a stream and continue beating until mixture is thick and pale, about 3 minutes.

❖ Transfer the egg mixture to the top of a double boiler. Whisk together the egg mixture, zest and juice, water, and salt. Set bowl over boiling water and whisk gently for 10 minutes, cooking the mixture until it thickens around the edge. Transfer mixture to a bowl to cool. Cover and refrigerate. Will keep, refrigerated, for up to 3 days.

makes 2 cups (16 fl oz/500 ml)

apricot-strawberry sauce

Serve with ice cream or sponge cake.

½ cup (4 oz/125 g) sugar

¾ cup (6 fl oz/185 ml) water

8 fresh apricots, pitted and chopped

1 tablespoon fresh lemon juice

1 cup (4 oz/125 g) chopped strawberries

❖ In a large saucepan, combine the sugar and water. Stir over heat to dissolve sugar. Bring to a boil and simmer for 5 minutes. Add apricots and cook mixture at a slow boil, stirring occasionally, for 15 minutes, or until apricots are soft and fall apart. Transfer mixture to a food processor and process until smoothly puréed. Pass through a sieve into a saucepan.

❖ Add the lemon juice to the saucepan containing the purée and bring to a boil. Add strawberries and simmer for 1 minute, being careful not to let the strawberries fall apart. Transfer mixture to a bowl, let cool, and refrigerate. Serve cold. The sauce will keep, refrigerated, for up to 3 days.

makes 1½ cups (12 fl oz/375 ml)

tiramisu

5 eggs, separated

¼ cup (2 oz/60 g) sugar

2 cups (1 lb/500 g)
mascarpone cheese

¼ cup (2 fl oz/60 ml)
dark rum

24 sponge finger cookies
(savoiardi/ladyfingers)

¾ cup (6 fl oz/180 ml)
very strong black coffee

½ cup (2 oz/60 g)
unsweetened cocoa powder

❖ Whisk the egg yolks and sugar until pale and thick. Fold in the mascarpone and rum. With an electric mixer on medium to high speed, beat the egg whites until soft peaks form. Stir one-third of the whites into the mascarpone mixture. Fold in the remaining egg white.

❖ Pour the coffee into a small bowl. Dip each sponge finger into the coffee for 1–2 seconds. Line the base of a dish with 12 of the sponge fingers. Gently spread the mascarpone mixture over the sponge fingers.

❖ Sprinkle with half the cocoa powder. Repeat with the remaining coffee, sponge fingers, mascarpone, and cocoa. Refrigerate overnight. Serve chilled.

port wine
gelatin mold

serves 8

2½ cups (20 fl oz/600 ml) water

½ cup (4 oz/125 g) sugar

2 tablespoons red currant jelly

2 tablespoons unflavored gelatin

10 fl oz (300 ml) port wine

◈ Place water, sugar, and red currant jelly in a saucepan. Stir over low heat until dissolved.

◈ Place gelatin and 2 tablespoons of cold water in a small bowl. Place the bowl over another bowl containing hot water. Stir until gelatin is dissolved.

◈ Add gelatin to jelly mixture. Stir in port.

◈ Pour into a large decorative mold, or 8 individual ½-cup (4-fl oz/125-ml) molds or ramekins, and refrigerate until set.

coconut jelly

*2½ tablespoons (¾ oz/20 g)
unflavored gelatin*

2 cups (1 lb/500 g) sugar

4 cups (1 qt/1 liter) hot water

*⅓ cup (3 fl oz/90 ml)
coconut milk*

*5 tablespoons (2½ fl oz/75 ml)
evaporated milk*

*few drops coconut extract
(essence)*

3 egg whites, beaten until stiff

❖ In a bowl, dissolve the gelatin and sugar in the hot water. Add the coconut milk, evaporated milk, and coconut extract; stir well.

❖ Place the bowl into a larger bowl (a stainless-steel one is good). Fill the larger bowl with ice.

❖ Fold in the beaten egg whites. The mixture will be thick and smooth.

❖ Pour the mixture into flat containers or ice cube trays and refrigerate for 2 hours, or until set. Invert onto a cutting board and cut into squares. Serve cold.

apricot fool

1 lb (500 g) apricots

1/3–1/2 cup (3–4 oz/90–125 g)
firmly packed dark brown sugar

1 cup (8 fl oz/250 ml) heavy
(double) cream

✥ Halve and pit the apricots, then thinly slice them. It
is not necessary to peel them. Set aside about 1 1/2 cups
(9 oz/280 g) of the apricot slices. Place the remaining
apricot slices and the brown sugar in a food processor
fitted with the metal blade or in a blender. (The amount
of sugar you use will depend upon how sweet the
apricots are.) Process until smooth. Taste, adding more
sugar if necessary.

✥ Using chilled beaters and a large chilled bowl, whip
the cream until stiff peaks form. Gently fold in the
apricot mixture and then 1 cup (6 oz/185 g) of the
reserved slices.

✥ Spoon the apricot-cream mixture into individual
bowls. Garnish with the reserved slices and serve.

filo-topped apple pie

serves 4

425 g (13¹/₂ oz)
can apple slices

¹/₂ teaspoon
ground mixed spice

¹/₂ teaspoon
ground cinnamon

sugar

1 oz (25 g) golden raisins
(sultanas)

1 sheet filo pastry,
about 18 x 11 inches
(45 x 28 cm)

15 g (¹/₂ oz) butter, melted

✦ Preheat oven to 425°F (220°C/Gas Mark 5).

✦ Drain the apple slices, reserving the juice. In a bowl, mix together the apple slices, spices, sugar to taste, golden raisins, and about 2 tablespoons (30 ml) of the reserved juice. Mix thoroughly, then spoon into a small, shallow ovenproof dish.

✦ Brush one side of the filo pastry with the melted butter, then tear it into pieces. Arrange the filo pastry over the apple slices, with the pastry buttered side up.

✦ Bake in the oven at 425°F (220°C/Gas Mark 7) until golden brown, about 15 minutes. Serve warm.

mango mousse

serves 4

1 lb (500 g) mangoes,
peeled

1/2 cup (4 oz/125 g) sugar

1 envelope
unflavored gelatin
(1 tablespoon/1/4 oz/7 g)

3 tablespoons water

1 cup (8 fl oz/250 ml)
heavy (double) cream

3 cups (12 oz/375 g)
raspberries (fresh, frozen,
or drained, canned,
unsweetened)

◈ Slice as much of the mango flesh off the pits as possible, being careful to capture any juices. Pass the flesh through a food mill held over a bowl. Alternatively, press the mango flesh through a sieve into a bowl. Add any captured juice to the bowl as well. Add the sugar and set aside, stirring occasionally until the sugar dissolves completely in the juices.

◈ In a small saucepan over low heat, stir the gelatin into the water to dissolve completely; do not allow to boil. Let cool for 2–3 minutes, then stir into the mango purée.

◈ Using chilled beaters and a large chilled bowl, whip the cream until stiff peaks form. Fold one fourth of the mango purée into the cream to lighten it. Then gently fold in the remaining mango purée just until combined. Spoon alternate layers of raspberries and mango mousse into 4 individual bowls or into a 1 1/2-qt (1.5-l) serving bowl. Chill for at least 1 hour before serving.

strawberries romanoff

serves 8

This eye-catching yet easy dessert is the perfect ending to a summer meal. You will need to prepare the berries at least 2 hours before you plan to serve them. The cream topping, however, should be made at the very last minute.

4 cups (1 lb/500 g) strawberries

¼ cup (2 fl oz/60 ml) orange juice, preferably freshly squeezed

2 tablespoons sugar

2 tablespoons orange-flavored liqueur such as Grand Marnier or Curaçao (optional)

1 cup (8 fl oz/250 ml) best-quality vanilla ice cream

2 cups (16 fl oz/500 ml) heavy (double) cream

❖ Remove the stems from the strawberries, then cut the berries in half lengthwise. Place in a bowl and sprinkle with the orange juice, sugar, and liqueur, if using. Cover and refrigerate for at least 2 hours or for as long as 8 hours.

❖ About 15 minutes before serving, remove the ice cream from the freezer and leave at room temperature to soften. Alternatively, just before serving, soften the ice cream in a microwave oven set on high power for 15–20 seconds.

❖ Using chilled beaters and a large chilled bowl, whip the cream until stiff peaks form. Beat in the softened ice cream.

❖ Divide the strawberries and their juices among 8 bowls or wineglasses. Top each serving with a generous amount of the cream-and-ice-cream mixture and serve immediately.

chantilly bananas

serves 8

The French term chantilly describes sweetened and flavored whipped cream—in this case, partnered with bananas. Praline cups or chocolate baskets make an attractive presentation, but small bowls can be used if you are short of time.

1 cup (8 fl oz/250 ml) heavy (double) cream

2 tablespoons dark brown sugar

1 cup (8 oz/250 g) plain yogurt

1 lemon

4 bananas

1 tablespoon fresh lemon juice

8 praline cups or choccolate baskets (optional)

❖ Up to 1 hour before serving, using chilled beaters and a large chilled bowl, whip the cream until stiff peaks form.

❖ In another bowl, stir together the brown sugar and yogurt. Gently fold the yogurt mixture into the whipped cream. Cover and refrigerate if not using immediately.

❖ Using a zester, remove the zest from the lemon in long, fine strips. Alternatively, use a vegetable peeler to remove thin strips of zest, then slice thinly. Finely chop about half of the zest strips. Set aside the chopped zest and zest strips separately. If not serving the dish immediately, tightly cover the zest and refrigerate.

❖ Just before serving, peel and slice the bananas. Place in a bowl and sprinkle with the lemon juice and the chopped zest. Toss gently to mix.

❖ Fold the bananas into the cream-yogurt mixture.

❖ Pile into praline cups or small bowls. If using praline cups, place on individual plates. Decorate with the reserved zest strips and serve at once.

lemon soufflé
pancakes
with raspberry syrup

serves 4

RASPBERRY SYRUP

1½ cups (12 fl oz/375 ml) corn syrup

1½ cups (6 oz/185 g) raspberries

1½ tablespoons lemon juice

PANCAKES

1 cup (5 oz/155 g) plus 2 tablespoons
all-purpose (plain) flour

3 tablespoons granulated sugar

1½ teaspoons baking powder

½ teaspoon salt

¼ teaspoon ground nutmeg

grated zest of 5 lemons

¾ cup (6 oz/185 g) ricotta cheese

6 tablespoons (3 fl oz/90 ml) buttermilk

6 tablespoons (3 oz/90 g) unsalted butter,
melted and kept warm

2 tablespoons fresh lemon juice

¾ teaspoon vanilla extract (essence)

3 eggs, separated

nonstick cooking spray

confectioners' (icing) sugar

fresh mint sprigs (optional)

For the raspberry syrup, combine the corn syrup, raspberries, and lemon juice in a small saucepan over medium heat. Bring slowly to a boil. Reduce heat to low and simmer very gently until a light, crimson syrup forms, about 20 minutes. Remove from heat and strain through a fine mesh sieve, pressing on the pulp to extract as much liquid as possible. Cover to keep warm.

For the pancakes, in a large bowl, stir together the flour, 1 tablespoon of the sugar, the baking powder, salt, nutmeg, and lemon zest. In a small bowl, combine the ricotta, buttermilk, butter, lemon juice, vanilla, and egg yolks. Whisk until smooth. Add to the flour mixture and whisk together until smooth. The batter will be quite dense.

With an electric mixer on medium speed, beat the egg whites until soft peaks form. Add the remaining sugar and continue beating until stiff peaks form. Carefully fold about one-fourth of the egg whites into the batter, then fold in the remainder. Do not attempt to make the batter completely uniform; a few streaks of egg white are fine. Cover and refrigerate for up to 1 hour.

Lightly coat a griddle or a large nonstick frying pan with nonstick cooking spray, then preheat over medium heat for 2–3 minutes. For each pancake, spoon about ¾ cup (6 fl oz/ 180 ml) of the batter into the pan, to form rough cakes about 5 inches (13 cm) in diameter. Do not crowd the pan. Cook until large bubbles form on top, 3–4 minutes. Using a spatula, carefully turn over the cakes and continue to cook until golden on the second side, 3–4 minutes longer. Remove from the pan and keep warm while you cook the rest of the pancakes.

Divide the pancakes among warmed individual plates and top with the raspberry syrup. Sift the confectioners' sugar over the top and garnish with mint sprigs, if desired.

glossary

artichoke

The large flower bud of a type of thistle, grown primarily in the Mediterranean and California. Pointed, prickly leaves (the bases of which are edible) conceal the vegetable's tender, grey-green heart. Artichoke hearts are also available in cans and jars.

arugula

Green leaf vegetable, also known as rocket. Its slender, multiple-lobed leaves have a peppery, slightly bitter flavor. Often used raw in salads.

basil

An intensely aromatic green-leafed herb, basil has a sweet-to-peppery licorice-like flavor that enhances tomato-based dishes and sauces, and Italian pesto. Fresh basil is plentiful in summer; dried basil is available in supermarket spice sections. Immerse freshly cut stems in 2 inches (5 cm) of water, cover with a plastic bag, and refrigerate for several days.

bell peppers (capsicums)

Bell peppers are mildly flavored, with a crisp, crunchy texture. Green ones are most common, but red, orange, yellow and purple peppers are also available. Bell peppers are an excellent source of vitamin C. Some varieties are dried and ground to make paprika. Choose firm, shiny, unbruised peppers; avoid those with wet stems. Store for up to 5 days in the refrigerator. Do not wrap in plastic, which will cause the bell peppers to become slimy.

butter, unsalted

For the recipes in this book, unsalted butter is preferred. Lacking salt, it allows the cook greater leeway in seasoning recipes to taste.

capers

Small, pickled buds of a bush common to the Mediterranean, used whole as a savory flavoring or garnish. The salty, sharp-tasting brine may also be used as a seasoning.

chiles

There are many varieties of chiles, both hot and mild. They are sold fresh; canned and pickled; and dried and finely ground as a spice. Hot chiles contain oils that burn eyes and skin, so always wear rubber gloves or protect your hands with plastic bags when cutting up any fresh chile.

chives

Long, thin green herb with a mild, sweet flavor reminiscent of the onion, to which it is related. Fresh chives possess a better flavor than the dried herb. Wrap fresh chives in damp paper towels, place in a plastic bag, and refrigerate. Use within 3–4 days.

cilantro (fresh coriander)

Green, leafy herb resembling flat-leaf (Italian) parsley, with a sharp, aromatic, somewhat astringent flavor. Popular in Latin American and Asian cuisines.

cream

The terms "light" and "heavy" describe cream's butterfat content and related richness. Light (single) cream, sometimes called coffee cream or table cream, has a butterfat level varying from 18–30 percent. If unavailable, substitute equal parts heavy (double) cream and half-and-half (half cream). Heavy (double) cream has a butterfat content of at least 36 percent. For the best flavor and cooking properties, purchase fresh cream, avoiding long-lasting varieties that have been processed by ultraheat methods.

fish sauce

Popular, pungent Southeast Asian seasoning prepared from salted, fermented fish, usually anchovies. It is used both in recipes and as a table or dipping sauce. Known by various names, including *nam pla* (in Thailand), *nuoc mam* (in Vietnam) and *patis* (in the Philippines).

hot-pepper sauce

Bottled cooking and table sauce made from fresh or dried hot red chiles. Many types are available. Tabasco is a well-known brand.

oil, olive

Many brands, varying in color and strength of flavor, are now available; select one that suits your taste. Extra-virgin olive oil, extracted from olives on the first pressing without the use of heat or chemicals, has the fruitiest flavor. The higher-priced extra-virgin olive oils are usually of better quality. "Light" olive oil has a paler color and milder flavor. Store in an airtight container away from heat and light.

olives

The fruit of the silvery-leafed olive tree, olives are either cured for eating or pressed for their oil. There are dozens of varieties, both green and black. The former are underripe, with a salty, tart flavor; they are packed pitted or unpitted in jars or cans. Pitted green olives are sometimes stuffed with red pimiento, tiny onions, or whole blanched almonds. Black olives, including Kalamatas and Niçoises, are ripe, with a smooth, mellow flavor. Buy them in cans, jars, or in bulk.

paprika

Ground from dried, mild bell peppers (capsicums), paprika adds a dash of red to stews, dressings, egg and rice dishes, and sausages. Imported sweet or hot Hungarian paprika is more pungent than the mild Spanish type. There is also a smoked type that inparts a rich, smoky aroma and flavor. Most supermarkets stock paprika in their spice section. Store in a cool, dry spot.

parsley

This widely used, bright-green herb adds a clean, fresh flavor and decorative color to almost any dish. Curly-leaf parsley is ruffled, with a slightly peppery taste; flat-leaf (Italian) parsley is more pungent. (The plant known as Chinese parsley is not a type of parsley, but another name for cilantro, or fresh coriander.) Select healthy-looking bunches that aren't wilted or brown. To store, rinse and shake off excess moisture. Wrap in paper towels, then in a plastic bag, and refrigerate for up to 1 week.

shallot

This diminutive member of the onion family is formed in the same way as garlic, with a head made up of more than one clove. Shallots have a milder flavor than most onions and need only quick cooking. Both golden (French) and purple (Asian) types are available. Look for firm, well-shaped heads that are not sprouting. Store in a cool, dry place for up to 1 month.

sumac

Sumac is a decorative shrub that bears bright red berries with an astringent, fruity sourness. The ground berries are a popular spice in the Middle East, where they are used to flavor sauces, salads, meat, and fish. Look for ground sumac in well-stocked supermarkets or in stores selling Middle Eastern ingredients.

tomatoes

When tomatoes are in season, use the best sun-ripened tomatoes you can find. At other times of year, plum (Roma/egg) tomatoes are likely to have the best flavor and texture. Small cultivars such as cherry tomatoes and pear (teardrop) tomatoes, both red and yellow, are also available. Tinned tomatoes, plain or with added herbs and flavorings, are very convenient for soups, stews, and pasta sauces.

vinaigrette

Literally "little vinegar," a classic French dressing or sauce for salad greens, vegetables, meats, poultry, or seafood. It is a combination of vinegar or some other acid, such as lemon juice, seasonings, and oil.

vinegar

Literally "sour" wine, vinegar results when certain strains of yeast cause wine—or some other alcoholic liquid—to ferment for a second time, turning it acidic. The best-quality wine vinegars begin with good-quality wine. Red wine vinegar, like the wine from which it is made, has a more robust flavor than vinegar produced from white wine. Balsamic vinegar, a specialty of Modena, Italy, is made from reduced grape juice aged for many years, taking on a rich, tart-sweet flavor, light, syrupy consistency, and the deep purple color of a fine old wine. Specialty vinegars made from cider, Champagne, or fruit are also available.

zest

Thin, brightly colored, outermost layer of a citrus fruit's peel, containing most of its aromatic essential oils—a lively source of flavor. Zest may be removed in one of three ways: with a simple tool known as a zester, drawn across the fruit's skin to remove the zest in thin strips; with a fine hand-held grater; or in wide strips with a vegetable peeler or a paring knife held almost parallel to the fruit's skin.

index

Page numbers in italics refer to photographs.

a note on measurements

U.S. cup measurements are used throughout this book. Slight adjustments may need to be made to quantities if Imperial or metric measures are used.

acknowledgments

The publishers wish to thank Nancy Sibtain for compiling the index to this book.

muesli pudd

salad barbec

soup vinaig

noodles pa

muffins poa

steak mari